MANCHESTER CITY
125 YEARS OF FOOTBALL

A PICTORIAL HISTORY

Gary James

MANCHESTER CITY
125 YEARS OF FOOTBALL

A PICTORIAL HISTORY

Gary James

in association with

First Published in 2007 by:
At Heart Ltd, 32 Stamford Street, Altrincham,
Cheshire,WA14 1EY
in conjunction with
Manchester Evening News
1 Scott Place, Hardman Street,
Manchester,M3 3RN
©2007 Manchester Evening News

ISBN: 978-1-84547-185-9

Printed and bound by Bell & Bain Ltd,
Glasgow

Contents

INTRODUCTION / 6

THE BIRTH OF CITY / 10

THE FA CUP / 16

SUPPORTERS / 40

PROMOTING CITY / 50

LEAGUE CHAMPIONS / 62

THE LEAGUE CUP / 78

EUROPEAN CITY / 88

THE MANCHESTER DERBY / 100

MILESTONES / 112

MODERN CITY / 140

Introduction

The history of Manchester City Football Club has always been fascinating. From its birth in 1880 as St Mark's Church side through to the managerial reign of Stuart Pearce, the Blues have always striven to represent the people of Manchester.

At times City have been the greatest side in the country, one of the best in Europe and a joy to watch; at other times they have made the easy appear difficult. Some years a highly successful season has been followed by one of failure, while at other times the Blues have overcome tremendous odds to turn defeat into major success.

During 2005-06, the Manchester City match day programme included my series of articles looking into the history of the Blues. These proved very popular with fans and, after careful consideration, the decision was taken to create this book looking at the 125-year history of the team from a pictorial perspective. I've taken the snippets of information documented within the programme, added my favourite City images, and generally tried to create an interesting, appealing book suitable for all ages.

Hopefully this officially produced book will bring back memories of star players, great games, and interesting moments form City's history.

As with any publication, there are a great number of people to acknowledge. Of course Henry Hochland and his team at At Heart Publications have worked wonders with this book and, as a City-supporting publisher, Henry understands the bond supporters have with the Blues. He also has great memories of City through the years.

A large number of former players, supporters and others have helped along the way including Peter Barnes, Chris Bird, Colin Bell MBE, Dennis Chapman, Brian Houghton, Alan Jubb, Richard Tucker and the present day staff of MCFC.

I am especially indebted to club photographer, Eddie Garvey, whose images of City over the last five years form a significant part of this book and help highlight the modern era.

Special thanks also go to the staff at the Manchester City Experience (the award-winning museum and tour) who have helped enormously.

Finally, a big thank you, as always, goes to my wife and children. Thanks once again for your support.

Gary James

and so the city of Manchester
was to be represented by Manchester City

"St. Mark's Church played a pivotal role in the club's birth and the vast majority of the early players lived in that area"

The Birth of City

In 1608 football was banned by the Manchester lawmakers because the game was causing too many injuries and too much damage to property. At that time football was very much a street activity and hoards of young people would charge through Manchester playing the game. It was very popular but the general rowdiness and the fact it was diverting interest from other activities, such as archery, raised concerns. As the nation needed its men to focus on military activities, pressure was placed on anyone who played the game.

250 years after this ban Manchester was growing at a rapid rate, particularly the areas of Gorton, Ardwick, Beswick and Clayton. Row upon row of terraced housing and industry was beginning to cover East Manchester, with new residents arriving from all over the British Isles and countries such as Italy, Germany and Poland. Religion played its part in trying to bind these new residents and in 1865 St. Mark's Church opened in West Gorton.

The church was located on what is now Gorton Villa Walk (ironically Gorton Villa were City's biggest rivals during the 1880s!), roughly where a Working Men's Club is today. This area is south of Ashbury's Station, and close to the Fujitsu tower about a mile from the City Of Manchester Stadium.

A short distance away at The Aces public house (named after the Speedway team), a blue plaque marks City's birth. Sadly, this is the only plaque marking City's history in Manchester and it would perhaps be more accurately placed on the Working Men's Club, or close to the Fujitsu building on Wenlock Way, as this is the most likely location of the club's first pitch.

By the late 1870s the area had significant social problems and the Rector of St. Mark's, Arthur Connell, worried about his parishioners. There were many issues of concern, including poverty, alcohol abuse, domestic violence and gang warfare known as 'scuttling'. Arthur asked his daughters, Anna and Georgina, to help engender a new spirit. Georgina focused on women's activities while her elder sister decided to tackle the men. With the help of significant figures at the local ironworks, Anna created a men's club and in 1879 a cricket team. Then in 1880 she created a football team, and the first reported game took place in November 1880 when St. Mark's (West Gorton) played the Macclesfield Baptist Church at home in West Gorton. Anna was clearly the key figure in the foundation of Manchester City and it is unlikely any other major football club can claim a female as its founder.

St. Mark's Church played a pivotal role in the club's birth and the vast majority of early players lived in that area. Even the great 1904 Cup final hero Billy Meredith lived on Clowes Street for several years, and he married in St. Mark's Church. During the 1970s much of this

THE
MONTHLY
MAGAZINE

St. Mark's
WEST
GORTON

PRICE FOURPENCE

JULY, 1959

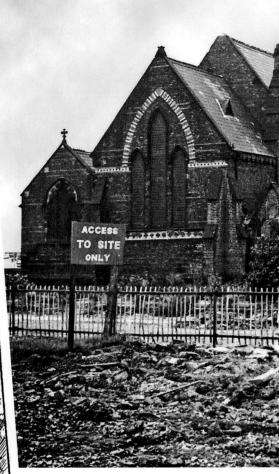

The parish magazine of St. Mark's Church provides this illustration of the front of the church

area was demolished and Clowes Street was re-routed (with Gorton Villa Walk taking the original route) when a new housing estate was built. Incidentally, Clowes Street took its name from the Clowes family who gave land for the construction of the church.

Within the Gorton area, the club played at grounds located at Pink Bank Lane, close to Redgate Lane, and at present-day Gorton Park,

the only former City venue still being used for football. A pitch was also rented from the original Bull's Head Hotel on the Reddish/Gorton border. With each ground move, the club grew and by 1887 St. Mark's had evolved into Ardwick AFC. By the end of that decade Ardwick had ambitions to become a major side.

At this time Ardwick were playing at a major football ground behind the railway arches at Hyde Road, next to Bennett Street. The old Hyde Road ground went on to stage a semi-final, inter-league games, and was City's home from 1887 to 1923. It was also the first

A rear view of St. Mark's, West Gorton, shortly before demolition in the mid-1970s

ENGLAND'S HOME

The first World Cup qualifying match ever played in England occurred in 1949 and was staged at City's Maine Road stadium. Maine Road was selected above Wembley as it had already staged some great internationals against Wales and Scotland during the 1940s, and it was felt Mancunians would provide a fantastic atmosphere for the game. They did, and the match ended in a 9-2 victory over Ireland watched by 69,762. Sadly, it was the last full international staged at the ground, but in 2004 England returned to City with two internationals at the City Of Manchester stadium.

This blue plaque is positioned on The Aces public house, close to Clowes Street in West Gorton. It marks the site of City's birth, but would be more appropriately positioned on the West Gorton Working Men's Club which now more or less occupies the site of St. Mark's Church.

provincial football ground to be visited by a reigning monarch when King George V attended a game in 1920. Crowds of over 40,000 regularly attended games there, and today the site is used as a storage area for container trucks. One of the stands can still be seen, however it is currently located at The Shay, Halifax, where it was erected after City sold it in 1923.

In 1892 Ardwick joined the Football League and football became Manchester's number one sporting activity. The first manager to guide the Blues in the league was Lawrence Furniss, who took charge for their first league season in 1892-93. Furniss was an ex-Gorton player and

This season ticket dates back to Ardwick AFC's first season of league football in 1892. This is the oldest known ticket connected with the Blues.

the man who brought the side its first trophy, the Manchester Cup, a year earlier. That first season ended with the Blues fifth out of twelve sides, but Furniss realised he was not a born manager and stood aside during the summer to allow a more outspoken man – Joshua Parlby – to push the Blues on.

Furniss remained a key City presence until his death in 1941. He became a City director and then chairman - the first of only two former players to hold that position (the other being Francis Lee) - and was also the club's first president. So important is Furniss to the club's history that in 1923 supporters campaigned to have the new Maine Road Stadium named in his honour. Furniss himself rejected the idea.

As St. Mark's had been formed in an attempt to bind the people of West Gorton together and to reduce some of the problems of the area, there has remained throughout the club's history a desire to represent the whole community. As the club grew, so too did this ambition. Then in 1894 Queen Victoria opened the Manchester Ship Canal and the whole city felt a great deal of pride in the achievement. It was a major moment for celebration and at Ardwick the football committee decided it was time to relaunch the Blues as a team to represent the whole of Manchester, and so in April 1894, Manchester City Football Club was born. The name was significant. Whilst almost any other name could have been chosen – Rangers, Rovers, Athletic, even United – none of those names felt wholly representative or even suggested there had previously been some sort of split, and so the city of Manchester was to be represented by Manchester City.

To help preserve the club's history and to remember former players and supporters, a memorial garden has been developed at the City Of Manchester Stadium. This features stonework salvaged from the club's first true headquarters, the Hyde Road Hotel, and a Maine Road Manchester City mosaic reconstructed by local artist, Mark Kennedy. These can be viewed by all visitors to the stadium throughout the year.

During the first thirty years or so of City's existence, newspapers would often illustrate matches by producing a cartoon of the game. This image illustrates City's 5-0 victory over Nottingham Forest in September 1905.

"The 1968-69 season had been tough for the Blues, but the FA Cup offered glory"

The FA Cup

CITY HAVE APPEARED IN THE FOLLOWING FA CUP FINALS:

1904 V BOLTON WANDERERS (1-0 win; wearing cambridge blue)

1926 V BOLTON WANDERERS (1-0 defeat; wearing cornflower blue)

1933 V EVERTON (3-0 defeat; wearing scarlet)

1934 V PORTSMOUTH (2-1 win; wearing maroon)

1955 V NEWCASTLE UNITED (3-1 defeat; wearing sky blue)

1956 V BIRMINGHAM CITY (3-1 win; wearing maroon & white stripes)

1969 V LEICESTER CITY (1-0 win; wearing red & black stripes)

1981 V TOTTENHAM HOTSPUR (1-1 draw & 3-2 defeat; wearing a deep sky blue)

City didn't really view the FA Cup as significant until the late 1890s. But once the Blues became an established league side, their confidence developed and their desire to find national success grew. In 1902 the Blues managed their first significant cup victory when they beat Preston North End 4-2 in a second replay.

Two years later City gained national coverage when, with inspirational captain Billy Meredith leading them, the Blues reached their first FA Cup final. Local rivals Bolton Wanderers were their opponents for the game at the Crystal Palace, prompting the national newspapers to focus on what they called 'The Lancastrian Invasion' of London. Stories talked of the 'strange Lancastrian dialect' of the fans – clearly the London journalists didn't understand that the Boltonian and Mancunian accents were somewhat different even then! – and on the provisions brought by the northerners. One newspaper held a stereotypical view of the Lancashire appetite for food and drink: "The trippers upheld the tradition of the North. Each

party seemed to have brought their own stack of provisions for the weekend. Nine gallon barrels of beer, stone jars of whisky and big baskets filled with 'baggins' were almost as plentiful as blackberries in Autumn."

City supporters wore sky blue and white coloured hats and rosettes while Bolton fans preferred bright umbrellas and 'white sleeved hats ornamented with trotters'. The fans were clearly the main focus in 1904 prior to the match, but the game itself provided one or two controversial moments.

Shortly before kick off one City player, 'Doc' Holmes, was so disgusted that he wasn't selected to play that he threw his boots out of

The FA Cup final squad is seen here in regular clothes prior to the final. Tough guy Billy Gillespie appears to have been given responsibility for looking after the club mascot, a small dog.

the dressing room window and made his views on the selection known to all who cared to listen. More controversy followed when a Manchester fan invaded the pitch to congratulate Billy Meredith on scoring the only goal of the game. According to one shocked journalist, it took five policemen to lead him off the field.

By far the most controversial incident was the goal itself. Meredith, football's first major star, scored from what Bolton claimed was an offside position. All Mancunians felt it was a valid goal, as did the referee and the media. In addition the Bolton players – apart from the goalkeeper - didn't appeal for offside at the

time. It was only afterwards that the incident was disputed and was debated at length in the newspapers of the day.

Nevertheless, the goal stood and the victory became the first major trophy won by either of the two clubs. City goalkeeper, Jack Hillman, kept the 1904 match ball, and it is known that for the following thirty years it was on display in the window of his tobacconist shop in Burnley. Unfortunately, it is not known what happened to it after Jack passed away in 1955.

Similarly, it is known that parts of the 1904 final were filmed and that this footage was shown in pubs and clubs in Manchester and Bolton on the

THE PLAYERS' ESTATE

During 1977, eleven streets were built close to Maine Road and named after deceased City players. These walks and closes still exist and are named after Horace Barnes, Eric Brook, Tommy Browell, Sam Cookson, Sam Cowan, Tommy Johnson, Jimmy McMullan, Billy Meredith, Frank Swift, Fred Tilson and Max Woosnam. In Trafford another street is named after ex-Blue Matt Busby, and at various grounds around the UK other former City men, most notably Busby, Don Revie, Bobby Johnstone and Joe Mercer have suites, stands or statues in their honour.

Prior to the FA Cup tie with Aston Villa the City players were photographed training at Southport. The Blues would regularly take a few days away from Manchester prior to FA Cup ties pre World War Two. The Southport air must have helped as City defeated Villa 2-1 at Villa Park on 19th February, 1910.

This 1913 FA Cup tie with Sunderland was abandoned after Sunderland's second goal in the 58th minute. The crowd had continually encroached the pitch and the referee called a halt when it was clear there were far more people in the ground than it was capable of holding. The official crowd was 41,709 but several thousand more appeared to be attending.

David Jack, after about 70 minutes, but the game was a closely fought contest.

As with 1904, the 1926 final was another controversial game, although this time the focus was on the stadium itself. This was City's first match at the three year old Wembley and the general view was that the stadium simply wasn't equipped to deal with major games. Over time these views have largely become forgotten – today everyone talks with affection of Wembley's first final in 1923 (known as the White Horse final and won by Bolton) and the chaotic scenes that ensued, but in truth there was nearly a major disaster that day. By 1926 the media and footballing authorities were not at all happy with the stadium and in the days that followed articles claimed the 1926 final would be the last at the ground. Everyone was fed up with Wembley's poor crowd control, not to mention the problem of ticket touts. This match was the first to see touting become a major concern after fighting broke out between the touts and the Lancastrian fans. In fact, the

Monday after the final. It's possible several copies were produced, and that one of these may be hidden away somewhere in the north west, however an extensive search of film archives has sadly found no trace of this footage.

More than two decades passed before the two sides met again in the FA Cup final. This time it ended in a 1-0 victory to Bolton. The scorer was

The 1904 Cup Final was the first time either of the Manchester sides had reached the final. Success by City over Bolton Wanderers brought the Cup to the city for the first time. Captain Billy Meredith scored the only goal of the final at the Crystal Palace.

City wore a darker blue than usual for the 1926 final against Bolton Wanderers. The shirt, described as Cornflower Blue at the time, was made by local sportswear company Bukta. Today Sam Cookson's shirt from the final is on display at the Club's museum, while this shirt, worn by Tommy Johnson, was bought at auction by a City fan and collector. The two shirts are the oldest known surviving City shirts.

police had to protect the touts from City and Bolton fans who felt they were being ripped off!

For City the 1926 final was again a major landmark. Not only was it the first time a Manchester side had played at Wembley, but the achievement was considered even more extraordinary because, at that time, the Blues didn't have a manager. Vice-chairman, Albert Alexander snr, had taken control of all team matters in November 1925, from picking the team to deciding on tactics. He guided City through every stage of the FA Cup run (including a semi-final victory over United), and had helped City achieve the record score in a Manchester derby (6-1 in the league at Old Trafford in January 1926). It was a truly great record for any man, let alone one who was vice-chairman and not a football manager.

In 1933 City reached their third final, but were defeated 3-0 by a Dixie Dean inspired Everton. After the defeat, captain Sam Cowan promised the Duke of York that City would return to Wembley next year and win the FA Cup. Few expected his prediction to come true initially, but those witnessing the Blues during 1933-34 soon saw determination running through the club with Cowan guiding his side through a series of record breaking matches to reach the 1934 final.

Portsmouth were the opposition, and their shrewd manager, Jack Tinn, ensured his players were in the right frame of mind for the final by bringing in leading entertainer Bud Flanagan (remembered today as the singer of the Dad's Army theme tune) to lessen the tension. In the City dressing room, however, the pressure of expectation was clear. Goalkeeper Frank Swift was particularly nervous. He had made his debut a mere four months earlier and had watched the 1933 final as a fan on the terraces.

Sadly, in the 27th minute, the Flanagan-inspired Portsmouth took the lead through Sep Rutherford. Swift blamed himself and at half time sat in the dressing room disconsolate. Yorkshireman Fred Tilson went over to Swift and said, "Tha' doesn't need to worry. I'll plonk two in the next half!"

Tilson was true to his word, although he did leave it late. His first goal came in the 74th minute while his second came in the final five minutes. As the final whistle blew to signal City's victory, Swift fainted. The tension of the day had simply been too much for him, but City were victorious and Cowan's prediction had come true.

Twenty-one years later, the 1955 FA Cup final saw Newcastle United beat City 3-1 at

Action from the 1926 FA Cup Final between City and Bolton. For this match the Blues wore a slightly darker shade of blue than usual to avoid a clash with the white-shirted Bolton. City lost the match 1-0 in their first appearance at Wembley Stadium.

1926-27 NARROWEST MARGIN

In 1926-27 with City desperate to return to the top flight at the first attempt, the final day of the season saw City in third place on equal points with second place Portsmouth. As only two sides were to be promoted the Blues had to better Portsmouth's result, and score plenty of goals to ensure their goal average was superior.

On the day City stormed ahead and eventually defeated Bradford City 8-0. This seemed to guarantee promotion and supporters raced on to the pitch to celebrate. However, the Portsmouth game with Preston had kicked off 15 minutes later than City's match. In those critical final minutes, Portsmouth's Willie Haynes netted his fourth goal and his side's fifth. That fifth goal proved crucial and gave Portsmouth a 5-1 victory but more importantly a better goal average than City. In the end Pompey were promoted by the narrowest goal average margin in history, leaving third place City an agonising one goal short of promotion. Portsmouth's average was 1.7755; City's was 1.7705. Interestingly, had goal difference been used in 1926-7 instead of goal average, as it is today, City would have been promoted and not Portsmouth.

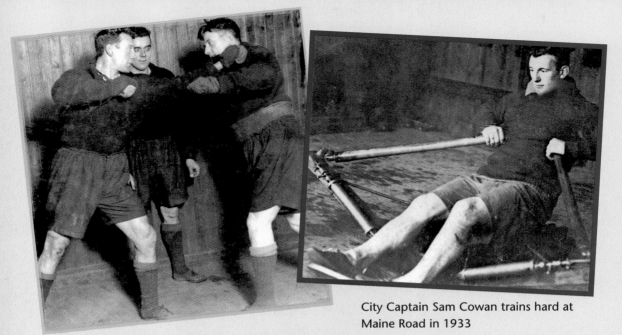

City Captain Sam Cowan trains hard at
Maine Road in 1933

Training 1930s style as Sam Cowan, Matt Barrass
and Len Langford enjoy a boxing session

THE WAY TO WEMBLEY
BROOK'S AMAZING SHOT BEAT STOKE

This cutting from the Daily Dispatch shows Eric Brook's wonder goal in the City-Stoke
quarter final at Maine Road. A record breaking 84,569 people attended the City victory.

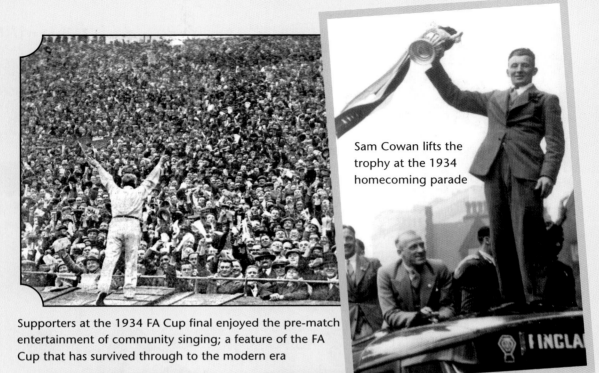

Sam Cowan lifts the trophy at the 1934 homecoming parade

Supporters at the 1934 FA Cup final enjoyed the pre-match entertainment of community singing; a feature of the FA Cup that has survived through to the modern era

The City players relax at Birkdale during their pre-cup final training stay in 1934.
Note the 19-year-old Frank Swift next to the large record player. When this photo was taken Swift still thought he would be replaced by the more experienced Len Langford for the final.

This cartoon depicts the action from City's 3-1 victory over Blackburn Rovers in the third round of the FA Cup at Maine Road

Bert Trautmann makes a save during City's 2-1 quarter final victory over Everton at Maine Road. A crowd of 76,129 attended.

Wembley. Newcastle had won the trophy in both 1951 and 1952 and were renowned as a great Cup side.

That year City made history by being the first side to walk onto the pitch for the final wearing tracksuits. It may seem a silly fact today, but at the time this was a major talking point. City's stars from the 1930s accused the Fifties' players of being 'soft', while the more style-conscious fans loved the fact that the team was setting new trends.

The game opened with City's Don Revie kicking off. City attacked but the ball soon found its way into Newcastle's possession and their captain Scoular ordered his men forward. Milburn hit a pass to White who managed a return and then forced a corner. White took the kick and the ball fell perfectly for Milburn, who headed the ball hard into the net after only 45 seconds. Milburn's goal held the record for the fastest goal in the FA Cup at Wembley until Di Matteo scored after just 42 seconds for Chelsea in 1997.

Worse was to follow as City's Jimmy Meadows suffered an injury in the 19th minute. He had torn his cruciate ligament, ironically in more or less the same location on the pitch as Walley Barnes' identical injury three years earlier for Arsenal, also against Newcastle.

The injury was a major blow and meant City had to play the remainder of the game with only ten men. They seemed to excel for a while and Bobby Johnstone, City's brilliant Scottish attacker, sent a powerful header home to make it 1-1. But in the 53rd minute, Bobby Mitchell gave Newcastle the lead, and then six minutes later future Blue, George Hannah, made it 3-1. There was no way back for ten-man City.

After the defeat, Geordie goal hero Jackie Milburn called for substitutes to be introduced for major games. He also stressed how impressive the Blues had been, commenting that, "for most people the gallant ten men of Manchester City won their hearts. Those players literally ran themselves into the ground. Ten wonderful hearts and a courage we shall always remember."

The following year, 1956, City reached the Cup Final again. It was a game that became memorable for the neck injury to Bert Trautmann, but it should also be remembered for good all-round performances from the entire City team. After the Newcastle disappointment the previous season, captain Roy Paul was determined that the club, playing in maroon and white, would beat Cup favourites Birmingham.

In determined style, City raced to an early lead. Don Revie, a late call up to the side, flicked the ball towards Joe Hayes who put in a left-foot

City return to Manchester with the FA Cup in 1956. This homecoming was the first outside broadcast by Granada TV who had launched just days earlier.

Joe Hayes pressures Birmingham's keeper Merrick in the 1956 FA Cup Final

shot and gave City the lead after two minutes and 47 seconds. Birmingham were rocked and clearly under pressure as City managed four corners in the opening ten minutes. Then, against the run of play, Noel Kinsey equalised and the match became more even.

City's tough guy Dave Ewing then decided to wind up the Birmingham players by singing 'Keep Right Onto The End Of The Road' throughout the game. The song had been adopted by the Birmingham fans throughout the Cup run and Ewing sang it whenever he took the ball from one of their players.

The score remained 1-1 at the interval and neutrals believed Birmingham would prove their worth in the second period, but Roy Paul was having none of it. He urged – some would say threatened – his team mates on and in the 65th minute Jack Dyson slotted past Merrick for City's second. Within two minutes Bobby Johnstone made it 3-1 and Birmingham were defeated.

Fourteen minutes from the end, goalkeeper Bert Trautmann dived at the feet of Birmingham's Murphy and was knocked out cold. Roy Little was almost forced to don the 'keeper's jersey for the rest of the match but Trautmann insisted he carry on. Then a few minutes later defender Dave Ewing collided with Trautmann, and the German was knocked out again. From then on Ewing played magnificently as he shielded the keeper from further pressure.

The game brought City their third FA Cup success, and thirteen years later their fourth arrived thanks to victory over Leicester City.

As League Champions the 1968-69 season had been tough for the Blues, particularly as influential captain Tony Book was out with injury until January. By his return it was clear

After scoring the second goal in City's 2-0 victory over Grimsby, Mike Summerbee entertained the crowd by swinging on the bar in celebration

City could not seriously mount a challenge for the title, but the FA Cup offered glory.

In the third round City defeated Luton 1-0 via a 26th minute Francis Lee penalty, and followed this with an exciting 2-0 victory over Newcastle in a replay (the initial game ended goalless). Alan Thompson wrote in the Daily Express, "they pulverised Newcastle so completely in the first half that it was not so much a match as a massacre. But all they had to show on the ledge was one early goal and half a dozen near misses."

The fifth round sent City to Blackburn, although the match had to be postponed on several occasions as a result of poor weather conditions and a 'flu epidemic in Blackburn.

City's 2-2 fifth round draw with Leicester in March 1966 prompted supporters to invade the pitch and Neil Young to copy Mike Summerbee's fourth round goal celebration

PROTESTING...

EXHORTING...

THREATENING...

... or just disgusted, Allison is as involved

When the game eventually did take place, sixteen days after the planned date, City dominated. The first goal came in the thirteenth minute when Francis Lee charged up field and knocked the ball past Adam Blacklaw and into the Blackburn goal. In the 47th minute the home side equalised, but eleven minutes later Tony Coleman restored the lead, later enthusing, "I'll never forget it if I live to be 100. I hit it with my right foot and it went in like a rocket. That hasn't happened very often!"

City went on to win the match 4-1, and next beat Tottenham 1-0 at Maine

When City faced Grimsby in the FA Cup on 12th February 1966 photographers focused on the role of Malcolm Allison in City's resurgence. The Blues won the match 2-0 and progressed to the quarter-final that season.

Road in the quarter final. The early moments of the semi against Everton were rather mixed, with City appearing nervous. Nevertheless, City, playing in their recently adopted AC Milan style away strip, ran and fought for everything and managed to keep Everton at bay.

Despite City's attacking nature, the game remained goalless right up to the last minute. Then a wonder goal by youngster Tommy Booth set the Blues up for their seventh Cup Final. The ball had been cleared by Harry Dowd and was worked upfield in a fluent passing move which started with Young. He fed the ball to Bell before running upfield. Bell accurately passed to Lee, who sent the ball to Young. Quickly, he sent an absolute screamer goalwards, only to see it rebound off the shoulders of Everton keeper, Gordon West. The ball went out of play giving City a corner taken by Young. Doyle headed it down to Summerbee who flicked it across the goal face towards the awaiting Bell. Booth rushed forward and sent the ball crashing into the net. It was a great moment.

Norman Wynne writing in The People was pleased for Booth. "The game was moving with certainty to a replay until Booth came up with his last minute goal. It was fitting that the City

Neil Young scores the only goal of the 1969 FA Cup final

Francis Lee in action during the 1-0 FA Cup final victory over Leicester City

Mascot Paul Todd is introduced to Princess Anne by Tony Book prior to the 1969 final

Supporter and photographer Alan Jubb captured these rare colour images of the team arriving for the 1969 FA Cup final. For years players and officials have talked about Malcolm Allison smuggling a young mascot into the stadium, but here (far right) Jubb captured the moment. Paul Todd became the first mascot on the pitch prior to an FA Cup.

centre half should be the goal scoring hero of the day. He was the youngest player on the field, and also the best."

Allison was also full of praise for Booth: "What can I add to what's already been said about him? He was the man of the match before he did what he stopped Joe Royle from doing - scoring."

By reaching Wembley, City had equalled Arsenal's record of six Wembley finals - a feat which made City manager and ex-Arsenal captain Joe Mercer immensely proud.

The final itself was not viewed as a classic, although Goal magazine deemed it a great spectacle. "Manchester City go into Europe next season having won the Cup with a display not up to their pre-match promises but good enough to far outshine Wembley's last few Cup Finals. There is no doubt that Manchester can play much better than they did against Leicester, but in view of the occasion and what was at stake, they did enough to make the game 90 minutes of intensely interesting football. And Leicester, thought by many before the game to have less than a dog's chance, proved just how levelling Wembley can be. Indeed, had they taken their chances, it could have been a very different story."

"Both sides deserve much credit for being prepared to attack at the risk of leaving gaps at the back. Manchester won because they were more fluid going forward and better able to cover their tracks when Leicester got possession. Now Leicester face the massive task of guaranteeing First Division safety. They have enough problems without pausing to consider the omen that Manchester City were relegated in 1926 having lost the Cup Final 1-0 to Bolton. But whatever happens to Leicester - and there is no doubt that for most of the team, reaching Wembley would be no consolation for going down - they can feel proud of a Cup Final performance that drew loud applause from Manchester supporters as Leicester left the pitch. They realised that this Leicester side could have won had Neil Young not scored that fine goal just when Frank O'Farrell's team were looking to have the edge."

In terms of action it had been fairly close. Early on Leicester's Allan Clarke, at that time the most expensive player in Britain at £150,000, had a superb shot which Dowd finger tipped to safety. Then both Young and Coleman saw attempts miss their target as City tried to seize the initiative. The goal came after 23 minutes when Summerbee gathered a throw-in from Lee, raced down the right, slipped past Leicester player David Nish and centred the ball to Neil Young. The City striker crashed the ball past the England under-23 goalkeeper, Peter Shilton, and into the top corner with his left foot. Young knew he had scored from the second he hit the ball.

Young, the scorer, later commented to reporters, "in these situations you don't have time to aim for a particular spot. You just sense

Images from the 1969 FA Cup Final

the chance, hit it, and hope for the best. I thought I did everything right with my first chance, but it went over and the same could have happened when I scored."

The match ended 1-0 and Leicester did go on to combine defeat with relegation, thereby emulating City's feat of 1926. Tony Book: "I thought we played very well early on. We lost a little after our goal. But we created more chances overall and I never had any real doubts."

Joe Mercer: "We were determined to play attractive football and before the boys went out they were told to give the public a display they'd remember. I think they succeeded." After the game Mercer stood on the pitch laughing and joking with Malcolm Allison.

They also conducted the fans' singing for a while. It was one of the best moments during the successful partnership and, while the celebrations continued, Allison turned to Mercer and said, "Boss, I'm worried." Mercer was puzzled; the FA Cup was City's fourth trophy win since 1966, after the League Cup, the Charity Shield, and the Second Division Championship. He asked Allison for an explanation. Allison laughed, "Well, Boss, I can't help wondering what went wrong in 1967 when we didn't win anything!"

The 1969 homecoming was a bit unusual as the Blues decided to start their tour of the city at Wilmslow, where kit manufacturer Umbro was based. 25,000 people turned out in Wilmslow town centre at the start of the 12-mile trip to Albert Square in Manchester, where one

Tony Book wakes up the morning after the FA Cup win with a prized possession – the FA Cup

This was the first published colour photograph from the 1969 FA Cup final. It shows captain, Tony Book, surrounded by players Tony Coleman, Tommy Booth, Glyn Pardoe and Dave Connor.

newspaper estimated there were at least 250,000 people waiting to welcome home their heroes. The bus driver, Bob Jackson, who had driven Manchester United through the streets after their European Cup success twelve months earlier, found City's homecoming moving: "It was fantastic. I would say there were more people about than for United's homecoming, and I was very proud to be in the procession. I saw the game on telly and enjoyed every minute of it."

Twelve years later City played in their next FA Cup final. This, perhaps the most famous Cup

replay of all, was the 1981 FA Cup Final against Tottenham Hotspur. Everybody claimed the odds were against City with commentators focusing on the omens surrounding Spurs, like the fact it was the Chinese year of the cockerel.

During the game, Bond's men applied a great deal of pressure and Tommy Hutchison's header gave City a 29th minute lead. As the final progressed the Blues seemed to have total control with Gerry Gow and Bobby McDonald snuffing out the likes of Ardiles, Crooks and Hoddle. Then in the 80th minute Gow made a rather desperate attack on Ardiles. A free-kick was awarded. Ardiles tapped the ball to Hoddle who curled it around City's wall. Goalkeeper Corrigan appeared to have the shot covered, but Hutchison somehow got in the way and the ball hit his shoulder and was diverted into the net. It was the most agonising moment ever witnessed in a City final.

The Blues drew 1-1 with Spurs and the following Thursday Tottenham seemed more

More rare colour images from Alan Jubb's collection. These show the players collecting the trophy and making their way towards the dressing room.

City started their homecoming in 1969 from Wilmslow train station. Kit manufacturer, Umbro, was based in the town and recognised the strength of support for City in this part of Cheshire.

Wilmslow

Joe Mercer and Malcolm Allison enjoy the success as the Blues travel back to Manchester

Mike Summerbee makes a speech at the 1969 civic reception while watched by manager Joe Mercer

The FA Cup is housed at Manchester Town Hall ready for the celebratory banquet in 1969

The 1969 FA Cup final was held prior to the end of the season, which meant the Blues briefly held the FA Cup, the Charity Shield and the League Championship all at the same time. This photograph, taken in City's boardroom, shows groundsman Stan Gibson alongside Captain Tony Book and the three trophies.

Manager Joe Mercer and Mike Summerbee at Wembley last year after City's F.A. Cup triumph.

Mike Doyle is chased by happy fans after City's victory over West Bromwich in the 1968 F.A. Charity Shield Match.

City captain Tony Book poses with the three trophies the club have won in the last three seasons—left to right; The League Championship Trophy, The F.A. Cup and the F.A. Charity Shield. Book himself shared The Footballer of the Year Award with Dave Mackay last season.

Can City make it four today?

The 1970 League Cup final programme carried these images from the 1968-69 season showing Summerbee and Mercer at the 1969 FA Cup final, scenes at the end of the 1968 Charity Shield, and the trio of trophies held by City in April 1969.

composed when the replay commenced. Ricky Villa netted a 7th minute opening goal for the London side and City had to work hard to find a way back. Steve Mackenzie fired home a spectacular 20-yard volley to equalise three minutes later – a goal that has officially been recorded as one of the best Cup Final goals of all time – but the game remained competitive. Hoddle began to impress most neutrals, despite Gow placing him under a great deal of pressure.

Five minutes into the second half Kevin Reeves netted a penalty to give City a 2-1 lead. It looked as if justice would be done, however in the 70th minute Crooks toe-poked an equaliser, followed just five minutes later by a Ricky Villa run past Caton, Ranson and Corrigan to give Spurs a 3-2 victory.

John Bond wasn't particularly impressed: "It was a good goal, but Steve Mackenzie's volley was unbelievable! I bet if Keith Burkinshaw had been in my place he wouldn't have said it was a good goal."

Every year this goal is shown as part of television coverage, but the game was memorable for so

City do their lap of honour following the 1-1 draw with Tottenham in the 100th FA Cup final

Tommy Hutchison is welcomed back to Manchester by supporters after the 1981 FA Cup replay

Gerry Gow is welcomed back by supporters after the replay

many other reasons. In terms of goals alone, Steve Mackenzie's twenty yard volley was another spectacular moment and a Cup Final goal worth remembering. At the time this was described as the greatest FA Cup final ever.

Since 1981 there have been many interesting and entertaining Cup games, but perhaps the most famous was City's 2004 replay with Tottenham Hotspurs. This highly memorable 4-3 victory at Spurs was described as the 'greatest tie of all time'. The Blues were down to ten men and trailing 3-0 at half time, but came back to win in style. The ball from this match is on display in the Club museum.

TOP SCORERS

Two players, Francis Lee and Tommy Browell, have ended the season top league scorer for the Blues on five occasions each. For Lee those five seasons were consecutively between 1969 and 1974. Despite this continuing success, Lee was transferred prior to the 1974-5 season, and then proceeded to score 12 goals in 34 games as he helped Derby to the League Championship. Irvine Thornley, Billy Gillespie, and Billy Meredith were each City's top league scorer on four occasions. Horace Barnes, Tommy Browell, George Wynn, Colin Bell, Uwe Rosler, and Shaun Goater were top scorers on three occasions each.

"Supporters have always played a key part in City's existence"

Supporters

Manchester City's entire history is wrapped up with stories of supporters and the involvement of ordinary Mancunians. Back in the 1880s, the club was created as a means to improve community spirit and as time moved on, the aims of the initial founders of the club have developed. By the early 1890s the club wanted to create a side for as large a population as possible, and in 1894, Manchester City was re-launched as a team for all Mancunians. From that point on City and its fans became a key part of Mancunian life.

During the 1890s, supporters wore fancy dress for several games at Hyde Road and would regularly bring bugles and other instruments to the ground. They created a party atmosphere and over the years that followed this approach has flourished, as have attendances at games.

City's first league ground at Hyde Road had a capacity approaching 40,000 for most of its existence, however its facilities were poor in comparison with some other leading venues, and even its considerable size was deemed too small by some. According to the 1905 Book of Football: "Naturally, with such a large population to draw upon, Manchester City get exceptionally big gates, and they would get larger did they possess a better constructed and more commodious ground. That is their chief want."

Despite such issues, Hyde Road crowd figures consistently reached 40,000 every season from 1904 to 1923. Had the move to Maine Road occurred around 1910 then it is likely attendances prior to 1923 would have reached in excess of 60,000.

Interestingly, when City did move to Maine Road in 1923, a fair comparison between City and United's relative pulling power could be made for the first time. That initial Maine Road season saw a league attendance of 58,159; only two Manchester derbies staged at Old Trafford had attracted larger league crowds. There was also a 76,000 plus FA Cup crowd at Maine Road that year; the largest attendance ever seen in Manchester for a football match at the time.

The Blues have always been a consistent performer when it comes to attendances. As early as 1895-96 the team was the third best supported side behind Everton and Aston Villa, while Newton Heath (Manchester United) were 21st. From 1898 to World War Two, City were

Billy Meredith and Max Woosnam, two of City's biggest former stars, took time out to respond to a young supporter's request for autographs. Interestingly, the tone of Woosnam's letter is as gentlemanly as the man's reputation always suggested, while Meredith seems keen to ensure his achievements are correctly recorded.

HERBERT THE FIRST

Although several former internationals had already appeared for the Blues, the first City player to appear for England while on the Club's books was 5ft 4in Herbert Burgess who, according to FA records, is the shortest full back ever to play for England. His first international came on 29th December 1904 in a 2-2 draw against Wales. Team mate Billy Meredith was in the side that day and had been a key member of the Welsh side for over a decade at this point. Interestingly, the Blues had already produced six Welsh internationals before Burgess' England selection.

Burgess went on to make four international appearances, and was followed by outside left, Frank Booth, and centre-forward, Irvine Thornley, who each gained one cap by April 1907.

never out of the top eight best-supported sides, while the Reds found themselves outside the top eight on twenty occasions during the same period, with their lowest position of 34th in 1931. That same season, United's lowest home crowd (3,679) was the lowest recorded attendance in the whole of Division One - a position City have never held.

Considering all divisions of football, City topped the attendance charts in 1911, 1915, 1928 and 1929, but were a top four best-supported side on a further 33 occasions spread throughout time, and pre-World War Two the Blues were a top six side on 30 occasions. Significantly, of those teams appearing as the top six best supported sides in 2006, only Newcastle and Chelsea come close to matching City's record. They both managed 28 top six appearances. Liverpool had 22, Arsenal 17, and United were by far the worst of those sides with only 10 top six attendance appearances over 43 seasons.

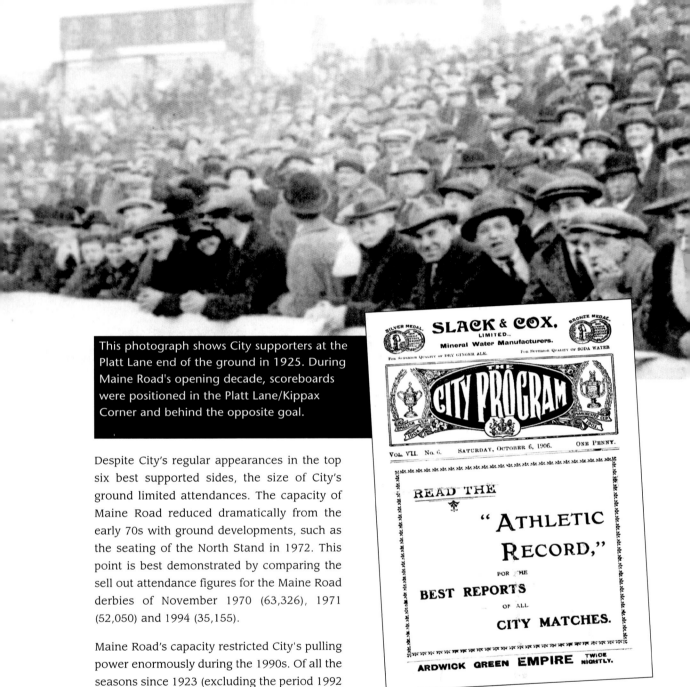

This photograph shows City supporters at the Platt Lane end of the ground in 1925. During Maine Road's opening decade, scoreboards were positioned in the Platt Lane/Kippax Corner and behind the opposite goal.

Despite City's regular appearances in the top six best supported sides, the size of City's ground limited attendances. The capacity of Maine Road reduced dramatically from the early 70s with ground developments, such as the seating of the North Stand in 1972. This point is best demonstrated by comparing the sell out attendance figures for the Maine Road derbies of November 1970 (63,326), 1971 (52,050) and 1994 (35,155).

Maine Road's capacity restricted City's pulling power enormously during the 1990s. Of all the seasons since 1923 (excluding the period 1992 – 2003, when Maine Road's capacity was its smallest), the annual average attendance was in excess of Maine Road's 1997 capacity on 40 occasions.

Interestingly, City's crowd has averaged above 30,000 on 48 occasions since the move to Maine Road in 1923, and out of the last 100

The City programme cover from the 1-1 draw with Preston on October 6th, 1906. In those days supporters didn't really save programmes, however this was the personal copy of player George Dorsett and has survived thanks to his family.

Bill Leivers is given the painted photograph treatment for this 1957 poster from Football Monthly

BILL LEIVERS (Manchester City)

BILL McADAMS
Manchester City
and Ireland

Throughout football history supporters have been keen to collect photographs and articles of their heroes. This cutting from Football Monthly shows a painted colour image of goalscorer Bill McAdams. Football Monthly, founded by ex-Sunderland man Charles Buchan, was a hugely popular magazine through to the 1990s.

Charles Buchan's
FOOTBALL
MONTHLY
OCTOBER
1957

1'6
Overseas Price 2/-
Forces Overseas 1/6

STAN CHARLTON
Arsenal
and
ROY CLARKE
Manchester City

Roy Clarke makes the cover of Football Monthly in October 1957. The actual photograph was taken at the Arsenal-City match of 6th October, 1956. Clarke scored twice that day, but the result was a shock…Arsenal won 7-3!

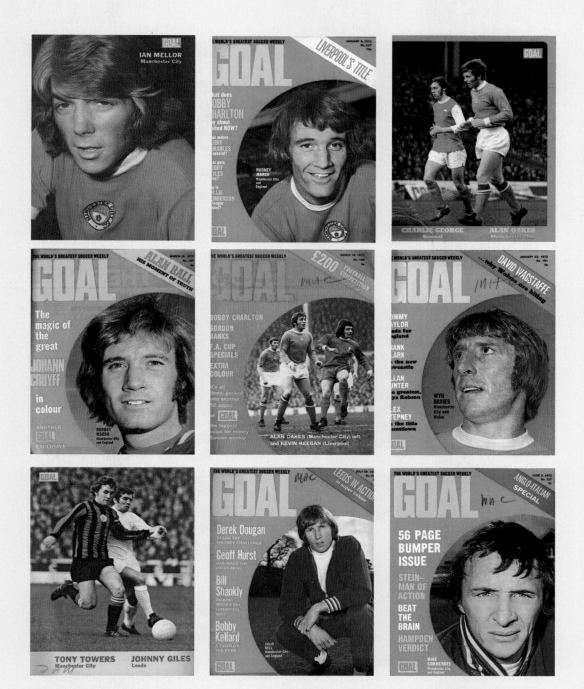

These pages and covers from the 1960s and 1970s cult magazine Goal covered City's star men. Goal was a very popular magazine and changed the style of football reporting. Whereas Football Monthly had always treated the game seriously, Goal tried to liven its stories up. Manchester City were regularly featured and the views of Malcolm Allison and players such as Mike Summerbee, Francis Lee and Rodney Marsh were often sought.

Dissatisfaction at the state of City in 1965 led to a group of 'rebels' challenging the direction of the club. These rebels issued a ten point plan which in itself prompted a response from chief scout, Harry Godwin.

Supporter Colin Meadows hit the headlines in October 1965 after leaving his home and a good job in the south to become a vacuum cleaner salesman in Manchester. The reason he packed it all in? He was desperate to be near his beloved Blues.

years the Blues have attracted average crowds of less than 20,000 just five times.

For many clubs, success, or lack of it, has the biggest impact on support. This briefly affected City during the early 1960s, however the biggest negative factor affecting the club's attendances appears to be the transfer of players. In 1930, crowds dropped by a staggering 8,000 as a direct result of cult hero Tommy Johnson being sold to Everton. Supporters were livid and boycotted games as a result. It took five seasons and consecutive FA Cup final appearances for attendances to return to their regular level.

Similarly in 1982, the transfer of Trevor Francis caused attendances to drop from 34,063 to 26,789. In fact, crowd figures didn't return to their pre-1982 level until 2000, although the return of Francis Lee as chairman saw crowds jump by 5,000 in 1994 and Maine Road was more or less at capacity from then until demolition despite significant struggles.

During the 1980s, supporters livened up Second Division matches with a return to the fancy dress and party atmosphere they had enjoyed ninety years earlier. Inflatable bananas were brought to games both home and away, while a famous game on Boxing Day 1988 saw over 12,000 City fans travel to Stoke carrying inflatables and dressing in fancy dress. The party atmosphere livened up the terraces, but once City achieved promotion that season the inflatables started to disappear. Success on the pitch was clearly what was needed most.

'DESERTED'

Part of Maine Road's lowest-ever League gate (8,015) yesterday.

This cutting from The Pink shows action from City's 2-1 defeat by Swindon in January 1965. This game made the headlines as it was attended by only 8,015 fans – the lowest official league crowd for a City game at Maine Road.

VERDICT ON CITY

OH, dear, City! That midweek Cup hangover remained at Maine Road today when the Blues, on top for almost 90 per cent of the game, failed to exploit the goal chances against a desperate Swindon side.

Jimmy Murray was again the main culprit, wasting two fabulous chances, one in each half.

Trevor Ogden was also at fault with his finishing, and the youngster, playing in only his second League game, should have made this match one to remember.

The Blues, at times, played some neat football, but their frustrated efforts at scoring left one wondering what is wrong with this side which on paper must be one of the best in the Second Division.

Swindon played a defensive game most of the time.

It seemed as though City would never score, and it took wing-half Alan Oakes to show the way.

So yet another disastrous home defeat plunges City into even further trouble, and the dreadfully low gate adequately sums up what the fans think.

Attendance: 8,015.

This supporter chose to recognise City's success on reaching the European Cup Winners' Cup final in 1970 by writing a song to the Blues

City fans queue against the North Stand for tickets for the FA Cup final replay with Spurs. The queue stretched most of the way around the ground.

Joe Corrigan and Peter Barnes were two of the biggest stars in football when this photograph was taken but, as with so many of the Club's truly great players, they always managed to find time to get out and meet the fans at social events and Junior Blues meetings

The Junior Blues rally at the Free Trade Hall. Within three years of its formation, the Junior Blues had become a major part of City life. In 1976 a rally was organised to demonstrate the size of the organisation. The Free Trade Hall was absolutely packed to the rafters and twelve months later a larger rally was held at Belle Vue.

WOT, NO CINDERS

Supporters have always played a key part in City's existence. In 1976 flower-seller Helen Turner was invited onto the pitch by the City players to celebrate their League Cup final victory over Newcastle United. Here Helen joins Joe Corrigan and Mike Doyle on their lap of honour.

No matter how big the star, City players were always keen to appear in the Club's annual pantomime at the City Social Club. Each year the likes of Francis Lee, Tony Book, Mike Summerbee and Joe Corrigan would dress up to take part in the panto staged for supporters. At the time of these features in Goal magazine, Lee and Summerbee were England internationals, and Tony Book had been the Football Writers' player of the year. Corrigan went on to represent England…how many modern day England internationals would take part?

"City supporters struggled to comprehend the importance of the goal"

Promoting City

City were founder members of the Second Division in 1892 as Ardwick AFC, and after re-forming in 1894 their first chance of promotion came in 1896 after finishing second. In those days, promotion and relegation were decided by a series of 'test matches', similar to modern day play-offs, although there was no automatic promotion/relegation of any description. The test matches were played on a league basis and unfortunately the Blues could only manage one victory, one draw, and two high-scoring defeats.

Despite finishing third in 1898, City had no chance of competing again in the test matches and, at the start of 1898-99, it was announced that the system would be replaced by automatic promotion. This gave City their best opportunity of promotion success.

There was a belief that anything was possible that season, and the second half of the year showed the club was moving forwards, especially when they defeated Darwen 10-0 at Hyde Road on February 18th. It was a thrilling game with Fred Williams netting five and Billy Meredith scoring the third of four hat tricks that season. The leading sports newspapers of the day were quick to point out that City's success was down to a team of hardworking individuals. There were no weak links.

Probably the most controversial – and popular - of all players during this period was the bustling Billy Gillespie. He was quite a determined character and had a habit of forcing the ball over the line any way he could.

GOALS IN A GAME

Four City players have scored five goals in a completed competitive match. They are: Fred Williams (vs Darwen in 1899); Tommy Browell (vs Burnley in 1925); Tommy Johnson (vs Everton in 1928); and George Smith (vs Newport in 1947).

Denis Law did however score six goals in an abandoned FA Cup tie against Luton in 1961. He also scored in the replayed game, but incredibly City lost that match.

He would often push the goalkeeper into the back of the net as well, in fact that was the part of the move he seemed to like best! It was a tactic criticised by opponents, but one that made Gillespie a cult figure on the Hyde Road terraces.

With Gillespie in outstanding form, the Blues were clear favourites for the Second Division title. They won their final four matches of

Another Channel-Flyer.

Following promotion in 1910, City struggled and ended the 1910-11 season in 17th place, narrowly avoiding relegation. As flying was still in its infancy, particularly cross-Channel, cartoons often used this theme to focus on City's fight to avoid relegation.

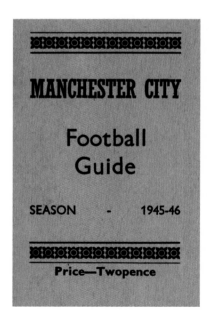

MANCHESTER CITY

Football Guide

SEASON - 1945-46

Price—Twopence

As peace-time returned, City issued a football guide outlining the state of the club and of football in general

1898-9 in style, and took the title for the very first time. It was also the first time either Manchester club had been promoted.

Six points behind the Blues was another relatively local team, Glossop North End, and the two sides became the first to gain automatic promotion to Division One.

As well as Gillespie, City's other stars included the legendary Welsh international Billy Meredith, unconventional goalkeeper Charlie Williams, Manchester-born Fred Williams, and the experienced former Preston idol, Jimmy Ross. Ross arrived just in time for the final nine games of the season but still managed to net an impressive seven goals. He was a player of true class, and had featured in every season since the league formed in 1888. In 1887 he scored seven (sometimes quoted as eight) in Preston's 26-0 Cup annihilation of Hyde. Ross's arrival was felt by many, in particular Meredith, as the turning point in City's fortunes.

In addition to promotion as champions in 1899, the Blues have won the second tier of English football on seven occasions: 1898-9, 1902-3, 1909-10, 1927-8, 1946-7, 1965-6 and 2001-2, and achieved promotion a further four times in 1950-1, 1984-5, 1988-9 and 1999-2000.

The most recent promotion came in 2001-02 when Stuart Pearce captained the Blues to the First Division Championship. The final match of the season was at home to Portsmouth. By that time promotion, and indeed the Division One Championship, was already assured. Manager Kevin Keegan's City defeated Portsmouth 3-1 with goals from Howey (9th minute), Goater (27th) and Macken (86th) on the final day of the season. Pompey's consolation came from Courtney Pitt in the 59th minute.

The Blues ended the season by equalling their record total of league goals – Macken's was the

The City team line-up from 1946-7, the year the side gained promotion as Division Two champions

This newspaper cutting from the Burnley promotion decider in 1947 shows City attacking Burnley at the scoreboard end of the ground

Supporter Dennis Chapman started collecting match reports of every game he attended during the war and as City reached their 125th anniversary of St. Mark's formation, he was still recording every game in the same way

The game that guaranteed promotion – five matches before the end of the season. City defeated Burnley 1-0 before 67,672 fans at Maine Road. This cutting came from the scrapbook of supporter Dennis Chapman.

Friendly persuasion

MERCER MEETS THE MAINE ROAD 'REBELS'

One of Joe Mercer's first priorities when he took over as manager in July 1965 was to reassure City's biggest stars that the Blues had ambition and a great future. Derek Kevan had been dissatisfied with progress pre-Mercer and the new manager worked hard to keep harmony at the club.

crowd incidents.

Two evenly matched sides played some attractive football in a no-holds-barred battle which neither side deserved to lose.

George Heslop was a tower of strength in City's rearguard where he was surrounded by heroes who kept a clever home attack at bay when all at times seemed lost.

Huddersfield added to their own frustrations by some atrocious finishing particularly by England class winger Mike O'Grady and hot-shot centre forward Tony Leighton.

City's best effort was a close-in effort from Ralph Brand which deserved a goal if only because of the way it was created.

Time for a rare breather. Time for Malcolm Allison to make one important point that could lead to two in tomorrow's top-of-the-table clash at Huddersfield. Players getting the briefing are (left to right) George Heslop, Mike Summerbee and Roy Cheetham. That man second from the right is Bob Russell.

Go, go, go . . and when Malcolm Allison shouts go you do go . . and you keep on going until he tells you to stop.

Irishman Johnny Crossan signed for City on 22nd January 1965. Crossan went on to captain the Blues to promotion in 1966 under Joe Mercer.

By October 1965, the media started to focus on the coaching ability of Malcolm Allison, pictured here putting a journalist through his paces

In July 1965 the first team picture of the Mercer-Allison era shows new signings Ralph Brand and Mike Summerbee

WITH THE COMPLIMENTS OF **Ty·Phoo** LTD., BIRMINGHAM 5
TEA

MANCHESTER CITY F.C.

Back row, L to R : Bacuzzi, Doyle, Ogley, Crossan, Gomersall, Young
Front row, L to R : Oakes, Wood, Kennedy, Connor, Pardoe

This Typhoo Tea card shows a City side from the early days of the Joe Mercer-Malcolm Allison partnership

Michael Hughes (left) and Gerry Taggart (centre) both appeared in City's 1988-89 promotion side, and together with Neil Lennon (right) went on to be selected for the Northern Ireland Under-23s team while at Maine Road. Although all three young players went on to make successful careers elsewhere, they were each allowed to leave City during the reigns of Howard Kendall and Peter Reid.

108th of the season – while the dying seconds also saw Stuart Pearce, playing in his last match, take the last ever first team penalty at Maine Road. Sadly, the penalty was missed, but afterwards Pearce was given a great ovation when he was presented with a trophy to commemorate his long and successful footballing career.

Three years earlier in 1998-99, City achieved promotion from the third-tier of English football. It had been the lowest the Blues had ever been, and the entire season was one of drama although there was a fiendish excitement in the stands.

A crowd of 32,134 squeezed into Maine Road for the Blackpool clash on the opening day, and the club and fans treated it like a Premier League game. The match ended 3-0 and it was an impressive performance at times, particularly from young debutants Gary Mason and Nicky Weaver, but there were also a few worrying signs. Despite the goals, City did miss quite a few clear chances and the general feeling was of relief that the side had managed to come away with a win.

Unfortunately the feeling didn't last, and a Kit Symons inspired Fulham defeated the Blues 3-0 on August 14th and Brian Flynn's Wrexham

As City pushed for promotion during 1988-89, high drama at Maine Road saw Paul Lake swallow his tongue during a collision with a Leicester player. Here the City players and referee call for Dr Luft from the Main Stand as physio Roy Bailey takes emergency measures to save Lake's life.

later frustrated City in a goalless match at Maine Road. The side dropped to fourteenth place following their next match - a controversial 1-1 draw at Notts County. It was the lowest position in the club's history and, for many, the result of a couple of strange refereeing decisions. Firstly, a highly debatable penalty had been awarded to County for an alleged handling by Horlock, then Pollock was dismissed for dissent.

After the County game, the Blues defeated Walsall 3-1, and then six days later Mel Machin's impressive Bournemouth side were beaten 2-1 at Maine Road. Apart from a 1-0 victory over Macclesfield, the following run of matches brought little comfort as the Blues drew four games and lost to promotion hopefuls, Preston.

Mixed results followed until Christmas and then City embarked on a twelve game unbeaten run which lifted them to sixth place. A 2-1 set back at Oldham – those that have watched the Blues for a long period would have recognised that as a potential banana skin! – was followed by a nine game unbeaten run. City were now in third place and on the fringe of automatic promotion. Sadly a 2-1 defeat at home to Wycombe and a 2-2 draw at Bristol Rovers ended that possibility, but a 4-0 thrashing of York on the last day guaranteed City third place in the table and a play-off against Wigan.

The first leg was played at Springfield Park, and became the last competitive match played at the ground. A crowd of 6,762 attended, but a more impressive figure of around 10,000

These scenes from the 1999 play-off final at Wembley between Gillingham and City show supporters celebrating the Blues' remarkable comeback. Note the presence of City supporters, Noel and Liam Gallagher from the band, Oasis.

attended Maine Road to watch via a large screen placed in front of the Main Stand. Sadly, the positive atmosphere at both venues was shattered in the first twenty seconds of the match as the normally dependable Wiekens and Weaver seemed to lose all sense of the occasion. They both stood motionless as Stuart Barlow rushed in between them to score a simple goal to put Wigan ahead.

Fortunately, Joe Royle's City no longer buckled in these situations and the Blues dominated the rest of the match. City attacked and attacked, and after 77 minutes finally scored the goal they deserved. Michael Brown made the goal with a good run down the right. He crossed to Paul Dickov, and City's powerful dynamo swept home a thoroughly deserved equaliser. The match ended 1-1 and the Blues felt satisfied.

Four days later Shaun Goater gave City a 27th minute lead in the second leg to send the Blues to Wembley for the first time since 1986. After the final whistle, thousands of supporters invaded the pitch to celebrate. It was a terrific sight and seemed to be the moment that ended years of hurt. Of course it wasn't, and with

Wembley around the corner no one quite knew what to expect, but it was a significant time.

The 1999 Play Off Final was played with City the clear favourites over Gillingham. In the end it was one of the most tortuous and at the same time joyous occasions ever experienced by Blues, and the entire day seemed to sum up exactly what supporting Manchester City was all about.

When the match kicked off, City were not the great force the media expected; instead they slipped their way across a wet surface and relied on 20-year-old goalkeeper, Nicky Weaver, to keep Gillingham at bay, particularly in the ninth minute when he palmed away an effort from Galloway. As the game wore on confidence grew and in the 26th minute a downward header from Horlock was superbly saved by Gillingham's Bartram.

Mixed play followed, although it is fair to say that City had the better chances and should have taken the lead, especially in the 75th minute when Goater side-footed a shot against the post. As the game progressed City fans became nervous, then with only nine minutes remaining, the Blues were dealt a major blow

Dickov celebrates scoring the equaliser in the 2-2 play-off final draw with Gillingham. City defeated the Gills via a penalty shoot out at Wembley Stadium.

Paul Dickov became a cult hero to City fans after scoring the team's equalising goal in the 1999 second division play-off final against Gillingham. This photo shows Dickov a few moments before scoring.

when Asaba toe-poked an evil shot into the roof of City's net. There was a feeling of huge disappointment in the stands, but worse was to follow as Robert Taylor made it 2-0 in the 86th minute. Two thirds of the stadium fell silent, then many, many Blues decided enough was enough and left for home. Those that remained were in for a treat.

With a mere 17 seconds of regular time remaining, Horlock side-footed the ball into the net, prompting those in the stands to believe that a draw could be possible. Four and a half minutes into injury time, Dickov fired an equaliser into the top corner. For a few seconds the stadium fell silent as City supporters struggled to comprehend the importance of the goal, and then wild celebrations erupted all over the stadium. Outside Wembley those that had left early heard the news and rushed back, and the stadium was full once more.

An extremely tense period of extra time followed, and then came penalties. The City players huddled together as a team, showing the unity that previous sides had clearly not enjoyed. This unity helped City win the penalty

There have been many father-son connections at City over the years. These include:

BARNES – Fifties Cup winner Ken was on City's coaching staff when his son Peter scored the opening goal of the 1976 League Cup final.

BEASTOW – William Beastow was one of the founders of St. Mark's Church side in 1880 and his two sons played in the very first match.

BOND – John was manager between 1980 and 1983 and he signed his son Kevin in September 1981.

BROAD – Jimmy was City's trainer from more or less the beginning of the club through to the 1920s and his sons became players. The more famous son, Tommy, was a star player between 1915 and 1921.

DOCHERTY – Tommy was United's manager when his son Michael played in two Manchester derbies for City.

HART – Hall of Fame Lifetime Achievement inductee Johnny was a great fifties star and '60s/'70s coach. His sons Nigel and Paul both became league players, and Paul has since had a good managerial career at a variety of clubs including Nottingham Forest.

HERD – Alec was a City FA Cup winner in 1934 and a major reason for the club's 1937 League Championship success. His son David found success at United, but spent his early life living on Maine Road in one of the club's houses. Both Alec and David played alongside each other for Stockport County.

MELLOR – Early '70s City man Ian 'spider' Mellor's son, Neil, is a present day league player.

MEREDITH – The first truly great City star, Billy, became the father-in-law of '20s City man Charlie Pringle. On 4th November 1922, the two men played alongside each other in a City league game for the first time, and the following season Pringle played in 49-year-old Meredith's last game, the FA Cup semi-final vs Newcastle.

OAKES – Alan is City's record appearance holder, and his son Michael is a goalkeeper famous for his career with Aston Villa and Wolves. Alan is also the cousin of City's youngest ever player, Glyn Pardoe, who in turn is now related to another '60s/'70s hero, Mike Doyle (Doyle's son married Pardoe's daughter, and Pardoe and Doyle now share a grandson).

SUMMERBEE – England international Mike entertained a generation; twenty years later his son Nicky was a key member of Brian Horton's side.

WRIGHT-PHILLIPS – Bradley is the son of former England international Ian Wright, and also the brother of ex-Blue Shaun.

City won the Division One League Championship in 2002 under manager Kevin Keegan. These scenes show the celebrations after the trophy was presented following their final match of the season against Portsmouth.

shoot out 3-1, but this score says nothing of the drama, the excitement, and the immense feeling of relief experienced at the time. Horlock, Cooke and Edghill netted for City, but the hero was without doubt Nicky Weaver who saved Gillingham's fourth attempt. The young keeper immediately went on a rather manic run across Wembley until Morrison and the other players finally dragged him back to reality. That penalty shoot-out will live with City fans forever.

Wild celebrations followed, with the players bowing to the supporters to show their appreciation of sticking by the club through an extremely difficult period.

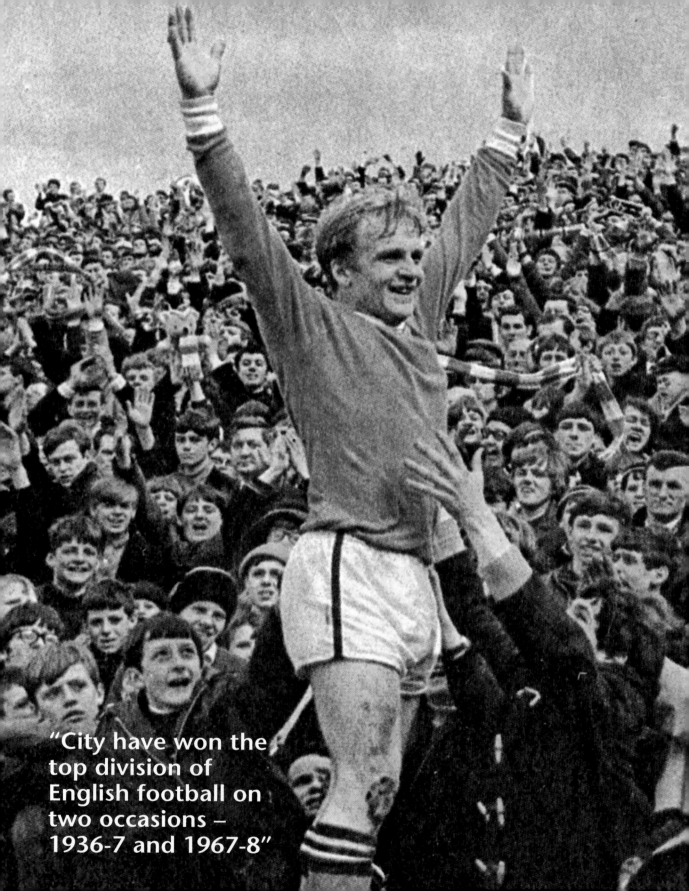

"City have won the top division of English football on two occasions – 1936-7 and 1967-8"

League Champions

City have won the top division of English football on two occasions – 1936-7 and 1967-8.

Even though the 1936-7 season is one of City's most successful, it is fair to say the Blues did struggle a little during the difficult early months of September and October 1936.

Despite exciting victories over Leeds (4-0) and West Bromwich Albion (6-2), an opening day defeat at Middlesbrough and another at Old Trafford in the first derby since United's relegation in 1931 caused a little concern amongst City's support. Further failures were yet to come, including a 2-1 defeat at Wolves.

A few exciting victories followed towards the end of the year, however, including a 3-1 win at Arsenal and a 4-1 win against Preston, but the real turnaround came at Christmas with a 2-1 home victory over Middlesbrough. A couple of draws followed, before a Maine Road crowd of 62,895 watched a rather dull but important return derby as City defeated United thanks to a solitary goal from Alec Herd.

In the next league game Toseland, Herd and Brook each scored as Portsmouth were defeated 3-1 at Maine Road. Two of the following three games were drawn, but the Blues had clearly developed into an exciting side as they ripped Derby, Wolves and Huddersfield to pieces in February/March. An excellent Good Friday visit to Liverpool thrilled City fans as the Reds were defeated 5-0 with goals from Brook (3), Doherty and Herd.

Three days later the return match saw the Blues go goal crazy again as they scored another five, including a seven-minute spell during the second half when they scored four. Liverpool did manage to pull a goal back, but the 10-1 aggregate score was a complete humiliation for the Merseyside club. Almost sixty years later Liverpool inflicted an equally humiliating 10-0 aggregate score over Alan Ball's City within a similar time frame.

Away at Brentford on April 3rd, City again found the goal scoring touch. Shortly after half-time the Blues were leading 3-0, but then, with the game seemingly won, the players seemed to sit back and in no time at all, Brentford had pulled the score back to 3-2. At a time when most teams would have panicked, City regained control and by full-time, the players had increased their lead to 6-2. Four days later, the Maine Road return ended in a 2-1 win, placing City second in the league behind Arsenal who were due to play the Blues three days later on Saturday April 10th.

For the early part of the match, City were easily outplayed by the Gunners, but in the 35th minute they seized control and took the lead. Arsenal's Bernard Joy sliced a clearance straight to City's Fred Tilson on the left wing. Immediately Tilson steered a long pass to Peter Doherty, who was being closely marked by

This image of City keeper Jim Goodchild in action against Tottenham Hotspur is believed to be from a meeting between the sides in 1920-21. That season, City beat Spurs 2-0 at Hyde Road with goals from Tommy Browell and Horace Barnes, and lost the away game with the same score.

Winning the League Championship in 1936-7 set the Blues up for a Charity Shield match with Sunderland in November 1937. In those days, the Shield was played at the ground of the Champions. The Blues beat Sunderland 2-0 on 3rd November 1937.

England captain, Eddie Hapgood. With Arsenal's keeper Boulton only a yard away and faced with a very narrow angle, Doherty somehow hooked the ball into the roof of the net.

Toseland scored a second for the Blues later in the match to give City victory and top spot in the table. With four games left, the club was confident that the title was at long last on its way to Maine Road. In mid-week Sunderland were defeated 3-1, then on April 17th the Blues played a memorable game at Preston. Both sides were missing players on International duty - City were without Sam Barkas and Jackie Bray - and the conditions were poor to say the least. The pitch was practically unplayable following heavy rain, and the Blues found it difficult to cope with the mud. After twelve minutes they were two goals down, and later in the half City's left-back, Robert Donnelly, was injured. With an obvious limp he moved into the outside-left position, while Eric Brook dropped back into defence.

MANCHESTER CITY'S AMOURS.

Manchester City, having been jilted by Miss English Cup, is wooing Miss League Cup with whole-hearted persistency.

This cartoon appeared in the City-loving Manchester Evening Chronicle. The Blues had been knocked out of the FA Cup two weeks earlier and were challenging for the League Championship. The gentleman with the flowers is supposed to be secretary-manager Tom Maley. Unfortunately, the Blues failed to woo Miss League and ended the campaign fifth.

Doherty and Herd kept switching positions hoping to fool Preston's Milne and Shankly, but the ploy was ineffective and abandoned prior to half-time. Early in the second half, with City very much under pressure, the tactic was tried again. This time it worked and Doherty pulled one back for the Blues. A minute later Doherty scored again, and then Alec Herd cracked in City's third goal from a Toseland centre. Within three minutes the game had turned upside down. In another attack, Doherty headed City's fourth goal of the game, also the club's 100th league goal of the season, and a little before the end, the limping Donnelly made it 5-2. With two games left, the Blues just needed two points to win the title.

At home to Sheffield Wednesday on April 24th, a crowd of 55,000 cheered City on to a 4-1 victory. At the whistle, thousands rushed onto the pitch in celebration. The crowd sang, shouted and cheered, until captain Sam Barkas, manager Wilf Wild and chairman Bob Smith appeared. Smith paid tribute to the team. "It has been a fine achievement, especially as they have not been beaten since last Christmas. On behalf of myself and my fellow directors, I take this opportunity of thanking the players. We are tremendously proud of them."

Wilf Wild was a very happy and proud man. During his five years in charge he had seen the Blues win the league and the Cup, and feature in another final. The final game of the season was away to Birmingham City, and the Blues were determined to increase their unbeaten league run to 22 games. With City 2-1 down

Mike Summerbee appears to be leading as City go pre-season training at Wythenshawe

inside the last couple of minutes it seemed as if the amazing run would end, but then came probably the most unusual goal of the season. Peter Doherty remembered the lengths he went to in ensuring City's record remained. "A high ball was lobbed down the middle, and Harry Hibbs, the Birmingham keeper, and myself raced for it. We collided heavily, and at the moment of impact, I fisted the ball through. To my complete surprise, a goal was signalled, and there wasn't even a murmur of protest. Nobody had seen the infringement. I was credited with a perfectly good goal, and our record was intact!"

CHAMPIONS DESERVE THE LUCK!

City's next championship came in 1967-8. That season saw a difficult championship race between several high profile clubs. Manchester City, Manchester United, Leeds, Liverpool and Everton had all demonstrated their strengths

throughout the year and such was the quality of those sides, that during the final weeks of the season there was little to separate them. Victories over Sheffield Wednesday, Everton and Tottenham helped City stake their claim on the title, and by the final match there were just three sides competing for the trophy – City, United and Liverpool. United were favourites, playing at home against struggling Sunderland, while City were playing away at mid-table Newcastle. City and United had 56 points, and Liverpool were on 53 with a game in hand, but the media assumed reigning champions United would retain the title. The BBC Match of the Day cameras went to Old Trafford where the League Championship trophy was also on display before the match.

The City-Newcastle match was a thrilling battle between two sides determined to win. Newcastle gave everything they could as they searched for victory, while City strove forward

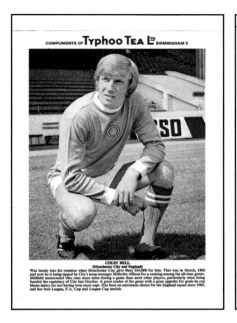

COLIN BELL
(Manchester City and England)
Was barely into his twenties when Manchester City gave Bury £45,000 for him. That was in March, 1966 and now he is being tipped by City's team-manager Malcolm Allison for a ranking among the all-time greats. Midfield mastermind who runs more miles during a game than most other players, particularly since being handed the captaincy of City last October. A great maker of the game with a great appetite for goals he can blame injury for not having won more caps. Has been an automatic choice for the England squad since 1969, and has won League, F.A. Cup and League Cup medals.

MIKE SUMMERBEE
(Manchester City and England)
Mike Summerbee originally signed for Swindon Town and is now a star of the Manchester City side who took the League First Division Championship in 1967/68. Highly regarded as a fine ball player, he has already represented his country against Scotland, Spain, and West Germany. The highlight of his career to date has been his selection for a place in the F.A. Canadian Tour side for Expo 1967.

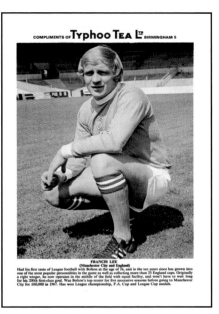

FRANCIS LEE
(Manchester City and England)
Had his first taste of League football with Bolton at the age of 16, and in the ten years since has grown into one of the most popular personalities in the game as well as collecting more than 25 England caps. Originally a right winger, he now operates in the middle of the field with equal facility, and won't have to wait long for his 200th first-class goal. Was Bolton's top scorer for five successive seasons before going to Manchester City for £60,000 in 1967. Has won League championship, F.A. Cup and League Cup medals.

These Typhoo Tea images of Colin Bell, Mike Summerbee and Francis Lee were highly popular during the late Sixties and early Seventies. These men were three of City's most talked about stars as the Blues won the league title in 1968.

in their customary attacking frame of mind.

Summerbee opened the scoring in the 13th minute, but Robson equalised two minutes later. Young made it 2-1 for City in the 32nd minute, but Sinclair equalised. At half time it remained 2-2 and coach Malcolm Allison later told the media: "I was going to go into the dressing room and give them a right old going over. But when I got there, I could see that they were all so tensed up. Instead I told them to go out and play as champions should play."

Without caring what was happening elsewhere, City attacked and three minutes into the half Young made it 3-2. Then, fifteen minutes later, Francis Lee scored a superb goal before jumping onto the perimeter wall to celebrate with the fans, a celebration that became the defining image of the Championship match.

Newcastle came back of course, no one expected anything less, and a goal from McNamee four minutes from time made supporters nervous, but not the players. Today everyone would expect the leaders to waste time, to hold the ball in the corner, or to send it wildly into the crowd, but at this match both teams fought on proudly. When the whistle came, news filtered through that United had lost to Sunderland, not that it mattered, and City won the title by two points. Liverpool won one of their games but lost the other and finished third, four points behind City.

The full City squad poses at the start of the Sixties. The first team players are, in the main, wearing City's traditional sky blue, while the reserve and youth team members are mainly wearing the yellow second strip popular during this period. Note Denis Law on the second row.

City pose for the cameras prior to their 4-2 league defeat by Blackpool at Maine Road on 2nd December 1961. The side was a mixture of experience and youth and ended the season twelfth in Division One.

The Manchester City squad from the 1965-66 promotion season

The 4-1 City victory over Tottenham on 9th December 1967 was a highly important moment during City's Championship campaign. The game, played in the snow, proved City feared no one and also proved to a national audience – the game was shown on Match Of The Day – that City were worthy contenders for the title.

The 1967-68 Championship winning season saw most of the City players become household names. At the end of the season the supporters made Colin Bell their player of the year.

Francis Lee celebrates his goal – City's fourth – as the Blues defeat Newcastle United 4-3 to lift the League Championship trophy. This photograph is the defining image of that Championship game.

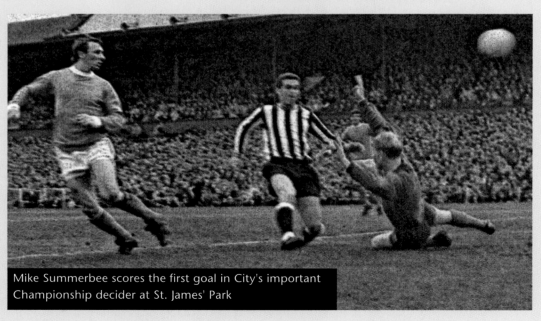

Mike Summerbee scores the first goal in City's important Championship decider at St. James' Park

Supporters invade the pitch after City's victory over Newcastle brings the Championship to Manchester. The City players are amongst this crowd somewhere, note the Newcastle player on the right.

Joe Mercer lifts the League Championship trophy at Maine Road prior to a friendly with Bury on 14th May 1968

Tony Book lifts the Championship trophy

Tony Book, followed by Ken Mulhearn, starts the celebrations at Maine Road

Supporter and photographer Alan Jubb found himself in the right place at the right time to capture these images of City's 1968 Championship presentation prior to the friendly with Bury. He even managed to get Malcolm Allison to sign one of them.

Francis Lee in action during the October 1970 meeting with Newcastle at Maine Road. Mike Doyle scored for the Blues in a 1-1 draw before 33,159 in the league.

Trailed by Burnley's Leighton James, goalscorer Colin Bell has control in the 2-0 victory at Maine Road on 19th April 1975

When City faced Wolves on 6th March 1971 Mike Summerbee returned to action following an injury that had prevented him from playing for four games. The game ended goalless at Maine Road before 31,987.

MANCHESTER CITY

Francis Lee and Tony Book discuss ways of combating the 'over the ball tackle', which was making the headlines in the early 1970s, and the 'two-footed tackle'.

These images were used as part of a series featured in the Manchester Evening News.

Malcolm Allison prepares the team for their customary team photo in 1979

Georgi Kinkladze celebrates scoring from the penalty spot as the Blues defeat Birmingham City 1-0 on 21st September 1996

"A tremendous homecoming parade followed"

The League Cup

City's first game in the League Cup came on 18th October 1960 with a 3-0 victory over Stockport County at Maine Road. Denis Law scored twice with Joe Hayes netting the other before a crowd of 21,065. A 2-0 defeat at Portsmouth followed in the next round. Three years later the Blues reached the two-legged semi-finals for the first time. Sadly they lost the first leg 2-0 at Stoke City's Victoria ground and Blue Derek Kevan netted the only goal of the second leg at Maine Road.

Six years later, during the 1969-70 season, City faced Manchester United in their next League Cup semi-final. This was the first season that all 92 league clubs had entered what had become a very popular and important competition.

The earlier rounds had seen the Blues defeat Southport 3-0, before a thrilling 3-2 Maine Road victory over Bill Shankly's great Liverpool side in round three. Goals from Colin Bell and Francis Lee ensured a 2-0 defeat of Everton in the next round.

The first leg of the semi took place at Maine Road before 55,799 fans. City opened well with a goal from Colin Bell after thirteen minutes and continued to dominate, but somehow United withstood the pressure. Then, early into the second half, Bobby Charlton equalised. The Blues continued to attack, knowing they had to use Maine Road to their advantage, and in the 88th minute Francis Lee darted towards United's goal. United centre-half Ian Ure stuck out a leg and sent Lee crashing to the ground. Inevitably Lee scored the resulting penalty, giving the Blues a 2-1 lead. As the players left the field George Best exchanged words with referee Jack Taylor and appeared to knock the ball out of his hands. The Irishman was fined £100 and suspended for a month as a result.

In the second leg, City youngster Ian Bowyer netted first, but the Reds fought back. Goals from Paul Edwards and former Blue Denis Law made the sides level on aggregate, but City were determined to win through. Eight minutes from time the Blues were awarded a free kick. Lee fired it at Stepney – perhaps aiming to outfox the United keeper – Stepney went to catch the ball, fumbled it and Mike Summerbee buried it into the net. Had Stepney avoided contact initially Lee's effort would have entered the net but been discounted. City won the semi 4-3 on aggregate in a tie described by Joe Mercer as "two of the most momentous games ever played in Manchester."

The final against West Bromwich Albion was played only 36 hours after City had returned to England from a European Cup Winners' Cup

A bubble gum card showing City at the start of the 1970-71 season

tie in Portugal. Freezing conditions had brought transport chaos and caused many to wonder if the Blues would be in the right frame of mind for the final. A fifth minute goal from Jeff Astle seemed to suggest that Albion would have the upper hand, however supporters needn't have worried as City took control. Francis Lee played arguably the best game of his career, while Mike Doyle slid home the equaliser in the 60th minute. Unfortunately, Summerbee was forced to leave the field shortly afterwards with a hairline fracture of the leg; an injury that would ultimately cost him his place in the European Cup Winners' Cup Final.

In extra-time Glyn Pardoe scored his first goal of the season to give City a deserved 2-1 victory and their first League Cup trophy. It also brought qualification for the European Fairs

Cup, the predecessor of the UEFA Cup. Interestingly, the competition only allowed one entrant from each city, causing Mike Doyle to joke, "That's not bad for my new campaign and car stickers – 'Keep United out of Europe'!"

Another four years passed before City reached their next League Cup Final in 1974. This time victories over Walsall (the game went to a second replay staged at Old Trafford), Carlisle, York and Coventry (played during power cuts with an electricity generator running loudly throughout the match), set the Blues up for a semi-final with Plymouth Argyle.

This time the Maine Road leg followed a 1-1 draw at Plymouth with Tommy Booth scoring a 65th minute equaliser so City already felt at an advantage. A crowd of 40,117 enjoyed a 2-0 victory over the third division opposition, with Lee scoring early on followed by a 48th minute delicately-placed goal by Bell. Unfortunately City lost the 1974 final 2-1 to Wolves, but two years later they were back at Wembley to try again.

The 1975-76 League Cup run started with a tricky 1-1 draw at Norwich City. The Maine Road replay was drawn 2-2 and led to a second replay at neutral Stamford Bridge. The Blues won that game 6-1 (Dennis Tueart scored a hat trick) and on October 8th they went on to face second division team, Nottingham Forest.

Unlike Bond, Forest's Brian Clough seemed pleased. "I was praying Manchester City would beat Norwich because I wanted to play the best. City are one of the most entertaining and talented sides in the First Division. When I last came to Maine Road it was with Leeds and we lost 2-1. If we keep the score down to 2-1 tonight then I think we'll show the strides that Forest have taken." True to form the game ended 2-1 with Bell and Royle netting for City. That result brought home a fourth round tie with Manchester United.

The United match was, in the main, a hugely successful night for the Blues, however there was also a great deal of sadness. City dominated the game and ran out comfortable 4-0 winners, but in the first half with the score at 1-0, Martin Buchan seriously injured Colin Bell in a tackle. The injury led to a long, difficult and ultimately futile battle to regain full fitness for the England international and, although he did return to the side, he was never the same player again.

Mansfield Town were defeated 4-2 in a tense quarter-final, giving City a two-legged semi-final against Jack Charlton's Middlesbrough. The first leg ended in a 1-0 defeat – Geordie-born Tueart was booed every time he touched the ball by the Middlesbrough fans – but a 4-0 Maine Road victory missed by Tueart, ensured City progressed to Wembley to face Newcastle United.

Alan Oakes and Glyn Pardoe prepare for extra time in the 1970 League Cup final. A few minutes after this photo Pardoe scored the winning goal.

City's average home attendance was 34,281, including approximately 15,000 season ticket holders. When tickets for the League Cup Final went on sale, the Blues had to think carefully about arrangements. Their allocation was not enough to satisfy their average attendance and secretary Bernard Halford took the unusual step of writing to all the other league clubs, apart from Newcastle of course, asking for any spare tickets from their allocations. Only two years earlier some tickets for the 1974 final had been put on open sale by the club.

This colour newspaper cutting shows Glyn Pardoe about to score the extra-time winner as City defeat West Bromwich Albion 2-1 in the 1970 League Cup final

In the eleventh minute of the final, a foul on Joe Royle by Glenn Keeley led to a free kick from Asa Hartford. The Scot sent the ball to Royle, who headed it down across the face of the goal. 19-year-old Peter Barnes stormed in to fire a half volley into the Newcastle net to give City the lead. It was a terrific opening goal, but 24 minutes later Alan Gowling scored an equaliser. City captain Mike Doyle pulled his team together and ensured the Geordies were kept at bay for the remainder of the half.

As the second half started the Blues looked for an early goal, which Tueart was more than happy to provide in the 46th minute. It was an incredible overhead kick, but the player later received some good-natured abuse. "I've never known so many people have a go at me for scoring a goal too early, because they were still at the toilet or queuing for a cup of tea! They couldn't get back in time."

For the rest of the match City remained in overall control, although Newcastle did have their fair share of opportunities. After the whistle the Blues

celebrated, although City's tough defender Dave Watson became the focus of attention in the dressing room as ITV's Brian Moore interviewed him while he was having stitches. Watson claimed his head injury was no more than a scratch, but the TV pictures showed otherwise and Watson's tough guy image was confirmed.

The Sunday Mirror made captain Mike Doyle man of the match for the way he guided his side through the game, while manager Tony Book became the first man to win the trophy as both a player and a manager. A tremendous homecoming parade followed.

Five years later City reached the semi-final again, however a highly controversial tie with Liverpool ended with a 2-1 aggregate defeat. The first match at Maine Road saw Liverpool win 1-0 before 48,045 after a Kevin Reeves' goal was disallowed in the opening minutes for reasons most neutrals found hard to believe. It was a devastating blow, and sadly City have not reached that stage of the competition since.

Tony Book is chaired by players Joe Corrigan, Francis Lee, George Heslop, Tommy Booth, Glyn Pardoe and Ian Bowyer after the League Cup victory in 1970 at Wembley

City bring back the League Cup to Manchester for the first time. This homecoming was City's third in two seasons.

Colin Bell, Ian Bowyer (12) and Glyn Pardoe celebrate as Pardoe's shot enters the net for City's League Cup winner in 1970

Rodney Marsh is introduced to the Duke of Kent prior to the 1974 League Cup final with Wolves

Goal heroes Glyn Pardoe and Mike Doyle join manager Joe Mercer to celebrate the 1970 League Cup success

Captain Mike Summerbee follows Ron Saunders onto the Wembley pitch for the 1974 League Cup final at Wembley

Tommy Booth and Derek Dougan tussle for the ball during the 1974 final

Denis Law celebrates with Colin Bell after Bell's goal in the 1974 League Cup final

When City defeated Middlesbrough 4-0 in the League Cup semi-final second leg at Maine Road in 1976, the goalscorers were Alan Oakes, Joe Royle and Peter Barnes. For some reason the other scorer, Ged Keegan, missed the opportunity of being on this post match photo.

Goalscorers Peter Barnes (left) and Dennis Tueart (wearing Newcastle shirt) flank tough defender Dave Watson after the '76 League Cup final

Mike Doyle lifts the League Cup at Wembley in 1976 following City's victory over Newcastle United

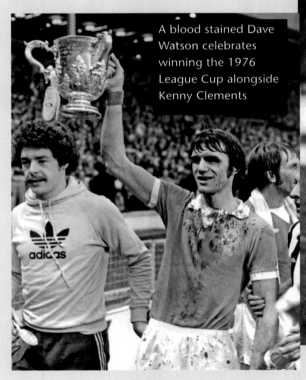

A blood stained Dave Watson celebrates winning the 1976 League Cup alongside Kenny Clements

Peter Barnes, watched by Joe Royle, keeps Newcastle under pressure

Dennis Tueart's memorable 46th minute overhead kick which gave the Blues a 2-1 lead in the 1976 League Cup final

"The Blues have competed in European competition in eight different seasons"

European City

The Blues have competed in European competition in eight different seasons – 1968-9, 1969-70, 1970-1, 1972-3, 1976-7, 1977-8, 1978-9 and 2003-4. Four of those have been as a result of trophy success, three as a result of league position, and one via the Fair Play League where good conduct brought a place in the UEFA Cup. Malcolm Allison, Tony Book, Kevin Keegan and Joe Mercer are so far the only men to manage the club in European football. Interestingly, Tony Book featured either as a member of the playing squad or as a manager in each of City's European seasons prior to the 2003-4 UEFA Cup run.

City's first European game was played on 18th September 1968; a goalless draw against Fenerbahce at Maine Road in the European Cup. As soon as the final whistle was blown, the opposing players celebrated like they had won the European Cup, and an extremely difficult second leg in Istanbul followed. A 2-1 defeat, played in an intimidating atmosphere, brought an early end to City's campaign. It was a major shock to a team that had dominated English football.

The following year, City entered the European Cup Winners' Cup as FA Cup holders. The campaign began in September with a 6-3 aggregate victory over Atletico Bilbao. In the second round, Belgian team SK Lierse were totally outclassed as City beat them 3-0 away and 5-0 at home in November. The third round wasn't played until March, with the first leg taking place only three days before the League Cup Final. The press expected City to rest their key players, especially as their opponents were allegedly rather inexperienced students, but Mercer and Allison were keen to ensure a good result.

A grim and at times difficult match ended goalless. A whole host of travel problems followed, disrupting preparations for the domestic final, but all of this was forgotten when the second leg ended in a 1-0 victory thanks to a goal from Tony Towers.

City's semi-final opponent, German side Schalke 04, had won the first leg 1-0 but City tore into them at Maine Road. Goals from Neil Young (2), Colin Bell, Francis Lee and Mike Doyle helped City to a 5-1 win on the night (5-2 on aggregate) before 46,361 fans. Keeper Joe Corrigan played with a broken nose. Three days after this win, Don Revie's Leeds United paid the Blues a major tribute by lining up prior to the Elland Road league meeting to applaud City onto the pitch. Mercer's men enjoyed the

Malcolm Allison was photographed with goalscorer Tony Towers after City's 1-0 victory over Portuguese side Academica Coimbra on 18th March 1970. Towers goal put the Blues through to the semi-final of the European Cup Winners' Cup.

welcome so much they defeated second placed Leeds 3-1!

The final against Poland's Gornik Zabrze was played in torrential rain on April 29th at the Prater Stadium, Vienna. In the twelfth minute, Neil Young gave City the lead, and shortly before half-time Francis Lee made it 2-0 via a penalty. Gornik's captain Oslizlo pulled one back in the 68th minute, but City remained in overall control. At the final whistle, the 5,000 Blues supporters celebrated wildly. City had become the first side to win a major domestic and European trophy in the same season. The team's fourth civic reception since May 1968 followed, as did a ten-mile tour of Manchester, starting at the airport.

The following season, as holders of the cup, the Blues progressed to the semi-final after once again facing Gornik in the quarter-final. The first leg ended in a 2-0 City defeat at Gornik. For this game the club had been

concerned about a number of issues and had even taken the unusual step of bringing their own food supplies to Poland.

After the match Malcolm Allison told the media, "we didn't play too badly, but nothing went right for us. We were all right at the back, but there was nothing coming up front. That was a great goal by Lubanski. The second one was a bit unfortunate. I know how good this Polish side is...they are much better than probably the general public appreciates. I would rate Lubanski as a world class player."

At Maine Road in the second leg, the Blues won 2-0 with goals from Mike Doyle and Ian Mellor. Mellor had only made his debut four days earlier and his achievements against Gornik immediately earned him a certain cult status amongst fans.

The 2-2 aggregate draw meant a replay was needed at a neutral venue. Copenhagen was selected and controversy followed. The Gornik President, Ernest Wyra, claimed City's players had used performance enhancing drugs at the Maine Road leg and his complaints caused UEFA to insist on drug testing for selected City players after the replay.

The game itself ended in a great 3-1 City win – Booth, Lee and Young were the scorers – and then came a controversial drugs test. Colin Bell, David Connor and Derek Jeffries were the three players whose names had been drawn to provide urine samples, but the players struggled to provide the sample. Orange juice was given to the men to help speed up the process but still no luck. Joe Mercer became extremely angry as the process dragged on and at one point he challenged the authorities and claimed: "It's an absolute farce. I am disgusted. What Gornik have done to us is scandalous and disgraceful."

How to greet a goal in the grand German manner

EVERYONE loves a goal . . . and no one more than the home fans. When Schalke captain Reinhardt Libuda scored the only goal of the first leg in Essen, the fans spilled over on to the pitch in a mad scramble to congratulate the hero of the moment. Mind you, if they got there they deserved to. They had to sidestep opposition such as guards and fiercely growling guard dogs!

DETERRENT . . . guard and guard dog.

Tony Book meets the Schalke captain prior to the European Cup Winners' Cup semi-final first leg in Germany. City were defeated 1-0 but won the second leg 5-1, however the talking point of the first game for one newspaper appeared to be the way the German authorities managed the crowd.

MOST CAPS

COLIN BELL appeared in 48 internationals, scoring nine goals, and is the most capped England international while with the Blues. His first international came in May 1968 and his last in October 1975. He also captained the side once and would, undoubtedly, have made many more appearances had it not been for the serious injury in November 1975 which prematurely ended his international career – he was only 29 at the time of his last cap. He also played in the 1970 World Cup finals in Mexico.

Centre-half **DAVE WATSON** appeared in 65 England games, but only 30 of these came during his time at City. He had an amazing run of 33 consecutive caps between 1977 and 1980.

TREVOR FRANCIS appeared in 52 internationals, but only ten while at Maine Road if we include the 1982 World Cup finals, while **FRANCIS LEE** made 27 full appearances within a mere 3 years & 140 days. He also scored ten goals from open play and, like Bell, he featured in the 1970 World Cup finals. In fact Lee was the first City player to play for England in World Cup finals when he faced Romania on 2nd June in Mexico.

Interestingly, **MIKE SUMMERBEE** was the first player of the great 1960s City side to play for England. He made his international debut in February 1968 against Scotland (1-1 draw) in front of 134,000 at Hampden.

Tommy Booth, Ian Bowyer and George Heslop celebrate winning the European Cup Winners' Cup at the rain soaked Prater Stadium in Vienna

Joe went on criticising the whole concept of drug testing, while Malcolm Allison took a more light-hearted approach to the affair. Malcolm arrived with a bottle of champagne, insisted on being allowed into the medical room, and then quickly returned, laughing, "They won't allow them to have this!"

In the end the samples were produced and the results came back negative, and so the Blues progressed. The 1970-1 semi-final brought a meeting with English FA Cup holders, Chelsea. An all-English semi-final was always going to be tough and sadly the first leg at Stamford Bridge ended in a 1-0 defeat but City remained hopeful of success. Then, after a gruelling run of games which included an important meeting with Liverpool 48 hours before the semi, a series of

Malcolm Allison lifts the European Cup Winners' Cup at Albert Square during City's homecoming in 1970

Francis Lee scores as City are defeated 2-1 at Windsor Park in the European Cup Winners' Cup against Linfield. Lee's goal ensured City progressed to the second round on the away goals rule after the first game ended 1-0 to the Blues.

Mike Doyle celebrates Francis Lee's goal in the 3-1 European Cup Winners' Cup quarter final replay against Gornik Zabrze in Copenhagen

Goalscorers Tommy Booth, Francis Lee and Neil Young celebrate City's victory over Gornik in the European Cup Winners' Cup quarter-final replay at Copenhagen

Manager Tony Book and Standard Liege's Robert Waseige are captured near the end of the UEFA Cup second round second leg match in Liege on 1st November 1978. City lost this game 2-0 but won the tie 4-2 on aggregate.

These two colour photographs by Alan Jubb capture the City side taking to the field at Maine Road in 1971 for the second leg of the European Cup Winners' Cup semi-final against Chelsea. The players seen are Francis Lee and Tony Book (plus mascot Paul Todd). The City keeper was Ron Healey.

Physio Roy Bailey and England international Colin Bell check out the conditions at the San Siro Stadium for the UEFA Cup game with AC Milan. The game was due to be played on 22nd November but was put back a day following extremely poor visibility at the stadium. Here Bailey & Bell are captured in the fog.

Paul Power scored in City's 2-2 draw at the San Siro in the UEFA Cup match played in November 1978

injuries gave the Blues little chance. Goalkeeper Corrigan was unable to play and was replaced by Ron Healey, while other influential players to miss the game included Tommy Booth, Colin Bell and Mike Doyle. Two minutes before half time, Healey diverted a swinging free kick from Chelsea's Keith Weller into his net. It was the only goal, but headlines from the two games claimed the semi had seen a marvellous performance from 'Mercer's minors'.

City's chance of becoming the first side to retain the trophy ended. Actually, no side ever

did manager to retain the European Cup Winners' Cup.

Goalkeeper Ron Healey remembers this time well. "Against Gornik, Joe Corrigan had played in the first leg and we lost 2-0 away and I think he got injured, so my chance came. We won the second leg 2-0 and the game went to a replay at Copenhagen. It was a great side to be in and, although I was a young keeper, I managed to get some praise. Then came Easter. I dislocated my finger in a match against Nottingham Forest and missed the first

Borussia Monchengladbach 3 - Manchester City 1. City's Kaziu Deyna leaves the field after City's 4-2 aggregate defeat in the UEFA Cup fourth round. Polish international Deyna had scored City's consolation goal, but this was to be the Blues last European tie until 2003.

City defeated AC Milan 3-0 (5-2 on aggregate) with goals from Asa Hartford, Brian Kidd and Tommy Booth in the third round UEFA Cup tie at Maine Road in December 1978

leg of the semi-final with Chelsea. We lost 1-0 away, but still had a lot of hope for the second. I came back into the side then, and sadly, I was at fault for the only goal – I diverted a free kick into the net! The next day I received some very, very bad press. That one mistake mattered and I did feel a very heavy burden for some time."

"There was a hunger for us all in those days. The win bonus would double your wage so we always went out fully determined. That bonus would truly change your week, and so you did all you could to win. Losing in Europe was bad because we wanted to progress, but I also felt guilty for losing the guys their win bonus."

UEFA Cup games against Valencia followed in 1972-3 (4-3 aggregate defeat), but City's next

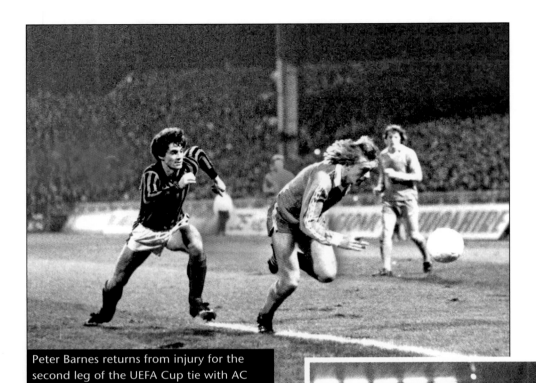

Peter Barnes returns from injury for the second leg of the UEFA Cup tie with AC Milan on 6th December 1978. City won the match 3-0 (5-2 on aggregate).

major European campaigns came in the late 1970s. In 1976 the Blues defeated Juventus 1-0 at Maine Road, but lost the return 2-0.

The following season saw City face Polish side Widzew Lodz. Prior to the match manager Tony Book – captain when City beat Gornik in 1970 – told the media he wanted a three goal lead to take into the second leg and, with about ten minutes remaining, the Blues were leading 2-0 and on top of the game. The goals had come from Peter Barnes and Mike Channon, and it seemed as if the players were already well on their way to fulfilling their manager's request and securing a place in the next round.

Sadly, everything changed in the final stages of the first leg. Dennis Tueart, a spectator on the night due to hamstring problems, later

commented, "we were 2-0 up with ten minutes to go and then Boniek scored direct from a free kick, followed by a penalty when one of their guys dived. Suddenly it's 2-2."

City captain Dave Watson exchanges pennants with Borussia's great captain Simonsen

The return leg was just as difficult. Tueart: "You go to Poland – it was an afternoon kick off – the pitch was awful, rock hard, and it was just one of those games. Nil-nil and they were happy because they were through. It was a lack of European knowledge that let us down."

Joe Royle felt partly responsible for City going out of the competition: "In the game I chased the ball down, challenged the goalkeeper, and the ball dropped. Whilst I was waiting for it to drop and then take it into the empty net I lost it. I should have volleyed it first time."

City went out of the competition on the away goals rule, but the following season (1978-9) saw the best UEFA Cup run of all.

Marvellous victories over FC Twente (4-3 on aggregate), Standard Liege (4-2 on aggregate) and AC Milan (5-2 on aggregate), brought City a fourth-round tie with Borussia Monchengladbach. Unfortunately, the return of Malcolm Allison between the Milan victory and the Monchengladbach game brought a change of emphasis at the Club, and the tie ended in a 4-2 defeat on aggregate.

Despite top-six finishes in the early 1990s, the ban on English clubs in Europe meant that City did not compete in European competition again until 2003-4 when Kevin Keegan's side competed in the UEFA Cup. Victories against Welsh side, Total Network Solutions (7-0 on aggregate) - the first competitive game at the City of Manchester Stadium - and Belgian team Lokeren (4-2 on aggregate) brought a meeting with Polish side Groclin. Disappointingly, that tie ended in a 1-1 draw in Manchester and a goalless game in Poland meaning the Blues lost the tie on the away goals rule.

"The Manchester derby is always played with the passion and force you'd expect from both sides"

The Manchester Derby

In terms of early football history, City and United faced each other in various friendlies and minor local competitions during the 1880s and early 1890s. The first significant meeting came in 1889 when Ardwick (City) faced Newton Heath (United) in an experimental game under floodlights at Belle Vue Stadium. Ten thousand people attended and money was raised for the victims of the nearby Hyde coalmine disaster.

Two years later Ardwick defeated Newton Heath in the Manchester Cup, making this the first significant trophy success enjoyed by the Blues. The Heathens had already found success in this competition and, as this was the first cup won by either of today's Manchester sides, it remains a very significant trophy.

The first league meeting between Manchester's premier sides occurred on 3rd November 1894 at City's Hyde Road ground. Sadly, a 5-2 Newton Heath victory gave the Heathens the points but according to the Umpire newspaper, it was the City players that were most impressive. "The play of Finnerhan and the young Welsh player Meredith was far superior to that of any other."

The following January, the Heathens won again (4-1) but the interesting point from a modern day perspective is that this game took place at the Heathens' Bank Street ground which today is covered by the grounds, most notably the car park, of the Velodrome across the road from the City of Manchester Stadium.

The Blues' first league derby victory came in December 1895 when league leaders City won 2-1 at Hyde Road. Promotion was missed in 1895-6 but did come in 1898-9 – a season that saw City defeat the Heathens 4-0.

Interestingly, City played their first league game of this period on Christmas Day 1896 against Newton Heath. The game was played at Bank Street and was attended by 18,000 fans – a figure described by the Athletic News as huge for Newton Heath. "The crowd was an enormous one and I never saw so many lads at a football match. They were really the cause of the encroaching in the first half, for they were continually creeping under the rails, and as a natural consequence their elders were bound to follow if they were to get a glimpse of the game."

Fans streamed on to the pitch on several occasions and the game was almost abandoned at half time. According to the Athletic News, "Mr J. Parlby of the League Management Committee told the crowd point blank that if they did not keep beyond the touchline, the game could not proceed, and the Newton Heath Club would have to suffer the consequences."

Parlby was actually a City director, and his words may have been influenced by the fact that Newton Heath were the better side. The game ended 2-1 to the Heathens.

It wasn't until 1906 that the two sides met in the First Division, following United's promotion. The first Division One derby ended 3-0 to City at Hyde Road before a crowd of 40,000 and by that time newspaper reports focused on the size of the crowd and the atmosphere generated at City's home ground.

SINCE THAT TIME THE MOST SIGNIFICANT DERBIES, FROM A CITY PERSPECTIVE, ARE:

1920 – three weeks after fire had destroyed City's Main Stand, the Blues defeated United 3-0 at Hyde Road. This game is significant as petty demands from United meant City had to soldier on at the badly damaged ground instead of spending a brief spell at Old Trafford. This was a major victory in Mancunian pride.

1926 – City defeated United 6-1 at Old Trafford to create the highest score in a Manchester derby.

1926 – 3-0 FA Cup semi-final victory for City at Bramall Lane.

1947 – Record derby crowd of 78,000 attend the first post-war league derby at Maine Road.

1955 – City 2 - United 0 in an FA Cup fourth round tie. City defeated Busby's Babes 10-2 on aggregate in three victories during the 1954-5 season.

1963 – A highly controversial and debatable penalty awarded to United causes a 1-1 draw and helps relegate City.

1968 – A 3-1 City win at Old Trafford helps City take the League Championship from the Reds.

1969 – A League Cup semi-final ends 4-3 on aggregate to City.

1974 – Denis Law's last goal in league football gives City a 1-0 win and helps relegate United at Old Trafford.

1975 – League Cup fourth round tie ends 4-0 to City, but Colin Bell's devastating injury causes much pain.

1989 – A 5-1 victory for Mel Machin's young City side over the Reds brings much pride to the Blues.

2002 – Maine Road's last derby ends in a 3-1 City win and sees Shaun Goater score his 99th and 100th goals for the Blues.

2004 – The City Of Manchester Stadium's very first derby sees City win 4-1.

2006 – United are defeated 3-1 at City.

Only one Manchester derby has been abandoned and replayed – the August 1960 meeting at Maine Road was abandoned after 56 minutes due to heavy rain. The score stood at 2-2 at the time.

Colin Bell and United keeper Alex Stepney in action at Maine Road in the 85th league derby. The game ended 3-3 with Mike Summerbee scoring the equalising goal in the last minute of the match.

The November '71 derby is remembered as a typical Manchester derby played with the passion and force you'd expect from both sides. In this photo, Francis Lee demonstrates to the other players the 'dive' he believed George Best had just made to try and gain a free kick. The crowd loved Lee's performance.

Francis Lee nets City's second from the penalty spot to make it 2-2 during the 1971 Manchester derby

Tony Book and George Best compete in the November 1971 3-3 drawn derby match

Action from the November 1971 Maine Road derby match. This was one of the last derby matches to be played without formal segregation and fences separating supporters on the Kippax Stand.

Colin Bell and Francis Lee during the 1971 Maine Road derby. Notice the original round badge won on the shirts that season.

Tommy Booth watches as Alan Oakes has control

Bobby Charlton seems keen to get play going again after Mike Summerbee is penalised. Summerbee's best man George Best looks on. When City won the Championship in 1968 Best joined Summerbee to enjoy City's celebrations despite the fact City had taken the Championship off the Reds.

Bobby Charlton and Colin Bell prepare for action while mascot Paul Todd looks on

Ian Bishop, Paul Lake, Trevor Morley and David Oldfield congratulate Andy Hinchcliffe after the player had just netted City's fifth in the 5-1 Maine Road massacre of Manchester United in September 1989

City celebrate after Hinchcliffe's goal gives City a 5-1 victory over United in September 1989

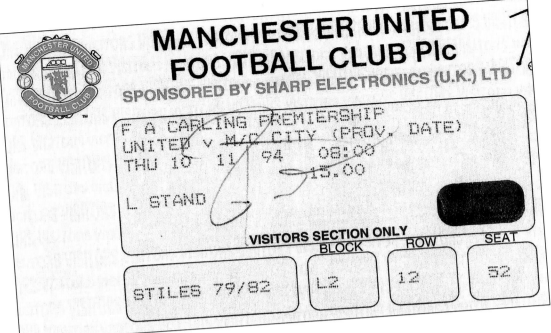

MANCHESTER UNITED
FOOTBALL CLUB Plc
SPONSORED BY SHARP ELECTRONICS (U.K.) LTD

F A CARLING PREMIERSHIP
UNITED v M/C CITY (PROV. DATE)
THU 10 11 94 08:00
15.00

L STAND

VISITORS SECTION ONLY

STILES 79/82 | BLOCK L2 | ROW 12 | SEAT 52

When the Blues were defeated by United (5-0) in the November 1994 Manchester derby at Old Trafford, City star Uwe Rosler, who was injured at the time, sat with the fans in the away section. His signature appears on this match ticket and is the only reason to remember the game.

The faces in the away section say it all as Shaun Goater nets his first goal in the 2002 derby which City went on to win 3-1. This was the last Manchester derby to be held at Maine Road.

The first Manchester derby at the City of Manchester Stadium ended in a 4-1 victory. The goalscorers were Shaun Wright-Phillips (top), Trevor Sinclair (bottom right), Robbie Fowler and Jon Macken (pictured far left).

Scenes of celebration from 2005-06

"Entertainer Rodney Marsh was signed for a record £200,000 in March 1972"

1865

St. Mark's Church, Clowes Street, West Gorton, was consecrated by the Bishop of Manchester on 30th November. A few days later the Rev. Arthur Connell was inducted.

1880

Rev Connell's eldest daughter, Anna, suggested forming a football team and two church wardens, Messrs Beastow & Goodbehere, formed St. Mark's (West Gorton) Football Club. The club played on waste ground near the church, and their first opponent was the Baptist Church from Macclesfield (2-1 defeat!).

1887

Seven seasons of name and ground changes culminated in the club renaming itself Ardwick AFC and finding a more permanent base between Hyde Road and Bennett Street in Ardwick. The club turned professional and paid existing player Jack Hodgetts five shillings per week.

1889

Ardwick played Newton Heath at Belle Vue in a floodlit charity match to raise money for the Hyde Colliery disaster fund.

1890

On 4th October Ardwick defeat Liverpool Stanley 12-0 at Hyde Road in the club's first FA Cup match.

1891

Ardwick defeated Newton Heath 1-0, with a seventh minute goal from influential captain Davie Weir in the Manchester Cup final. They also applied to join the Football League, as did Newton Heath. Both Manchester sides were rejected in favour of Stoke and Darwen. Instead Ardwick joined the Football Alliance.

1892

Ardwick, wearing their customary 'Cambridge Blue' (the colour may have been adopted by the club in the 1880s, though there's no actual proof), finished seventh out of twelve clubs in the Alliance and won the Manchester Cup for the second year running after defeating league side Bolton 4-1. The Football League was extended with the Alliance, in effect, becoming the Second Division.

1893

The Blues beat Bootle 7-0 at Hyde Road to put Ardwick at the top of the very first Second Division table. They ended the season fifth out of twelve, and were already established as Manchester's biggest crowd pullers.

1894

Financial problems beset Ardwick and after a dismal season (the team finished thirteenth out of fifteen in Division Two) the club collapsed. In April Manchester City FC was formed by the bulk of the Ardwick committee. They wanted to create a club for all Mancunians to support, and their ambition helped the club gain election to the league. The legendary Billy Meredith was signed and made his debut against Newcastle on 27th October.

1895

Ninth in Division Two. City Didn't bother to enter the FA Cup in 1894/5 and withdrew from their October 1895 qualifying round game with Oswaldtwistle.

1896

Second place in Division Two, but City failed to gain promotion via the test matches (similar to play-offs).

1897

Sixth position in Division Two. Defeated 6-0 by Preston in the first round of FA Cup in January.

1898

Narrowly missed out on the final year of the test matches, finishing third. The side reached the second round of the Cup but were defeated 1-0 at Bolton.

1899

Won the Second Division title on 56 points and, alongside second-placed Glossop North End, became the first side to gain

automatic promotion. Lost 3-2 to Small Heath in the first round of the Cup.

First Division One game ended in a 4-3 defeat at Blackburn, while the first Hyde Road Division One match ended 4-0 to the Blues.

1900

The first game of the new century was a friendly with Division Two's Newton Heath (Manchester United's original name). City won the match 2-1 before a Hyde Road crowd of 7,000.

The first league game of the century was a no score draw at Derby County. The Blues finished their first season in Division One seventh out of eighteen. They lost 3-0 to Aston Villa in a first round Cup replay. In September 1900 future Prime Minister A.J. Balfour attended Hyde Road.

1901

Eleventh in Division One. Once again couldn't pass the first round of the Cup (West Brom won the match 1-0).

1902

Relegated to Division Two, but managed to reach the second round of the Cup (losing to Forest 2-0). Former Celtic player Tom

Maley became the club's fourth secretary-manager during the close season.

Welsh international and key City defender Di Jones gashed his knee in the annual public practice match in August. Within a week he was dead; the wound had turned septic.

1903

Champions of Division Two for the second time. Top score was Billy Gillespie with 30 goals.

1904

Despite previous cup form, City won the FA Cup beating Bolton 1-0 via a Billy Meredith first half goal at Crystal Palace. Narrowly missed out on the League & Cup double, finishing second to Sheffield Wednesday.

1905

Hyde Road staged the 1905 FA Cup semi-final between Newcastle and Sheffield Wednesday. The Blues finished third (two points behind champions Newcastle). Aston Villa's Alec Leake accused Billy Meredith of attempting to bribe him to throw the Villa-City match on 29th April. Leake also threw dirt at City's Sandy Turnbull who retaliated by sticking two fingers up to the Villa

This cartoon highlights the benefit match for star man Billy Lot Jones that saw the Blues beat Middlesbrough 2-1 on 21st March 1908. A couple of points worth noting on the cartoon are: the role of trainer Bob Chatt who clearly had to carry off a few players at various stages; the blankets used to make a collection for Jones; the image of the railway engine. The old Hyde Road ground was overlooked by railway lines and clearly trains would often stop to catch a few moments of the game.

man. A full-scale enquiry was ordered.

1906

City ended 1905-6 in fifth place and then were mortified when the findings of the investigations following the 1905 Villa match resulted in the FA identifying financial irregularities at the club. 17 players, including virtually all the first team squad, were banned and fined; Directors Allison and Davies were suspended for seven months; and manager Tom Maley and chairman W. Forrest were banned from English football sine die.

When new manager Harry Newbould joined City in July he had only eleven players available. The club was virtually dead. Despite the problems, City won the first Division One Manchester derby 3-0 at Hyde Road on 1st December. New keeper Walter Smith was the star man that day.

1907

Manchester United made heroes of Billy Meredith, Herbert Burgess, Sandy Turnbull and Jimmy Bannister - the key City players forced out of Hyde Road. They were transferred to the Reds in December 1906. Most Blues were happy as it was seen as a good way to ensure the players remained in Manchester. It also helped City's then poor relations establish themselves as a force. Within four years Meredith and his men had helped the Reds win their first honours – two Championships and the FA Cup.

1908

Newbould's Blues managed to finish third with goalkeeper Walter Smith becoming the first City man to be an ever-present in all 44 league and cup matches.

1909

Inconsistency dogged Newbould's side, culminating in relegation at the end of 1908-9 on goal average. Bradford City were the team that survived by defeating Manchester United 1-0.

1910

City won the Second Division title – their third since 1899 – with a relatively consistent season: 23 victories, 8 draws, and only 7 defeats. The star man that season was George Dorsett who was top scorer with thirteen goals. His brother Joe joined City in August 1910.

Major ground improvements at Hyde Road resulted in three multi-span roofs being erected. This meant the Blues could provide cover for over 35,000, and have all four sides of the ground covered. The directors were quick to point out that Old Trafford, opened in February 1910, only provided cover for about a quarter of this figure.

1911

City played a leading role in the establishment of the Central League. Director W.A. Wilkinson chaired many of the initial meetings.

Goalkeeper Jim Goodchild signed in December. He stayed with City until August 1927 and was a firm favourite with the fans.

1912

The football world was stunned when United manager Ernest Mangnall – the man responsible for bringing the Reds their first successes and for the move to Old Trafford - announced he was leaving the Reds for the Blues. His final game in charge was the Old Trafford derby, played after he announced he was leaving. City won 1-0 and the Umpire newspaper summed it up nicely: "United speeded their manager rejoicing with two points to his new club."

1913

The cup-tie with Sunderland in February at Hyde Road was abandoned after crowd control difficulties. Many people were crushed. The official crowd was 41,709 but an estimate of 50,000 seems more believable, particularly as many ticket holders were locked out. Manager Ernest Mangnall was held responsible for the organisation of the day, with the Daily Dispatch claiming that he should always 'ensure mounted police are available to control the huge crowds that watch the City club'.

1914

City encouraged their players to join the armed forces and fight in the Great War. In addition, players and officials agreed to give 5% of their wages to the Prince of Wales' Fund.

1915

The Blues ended the 1914-15 season 5th, only three points behind champions Everton (interestingly Everton were also champions in the last season before WWII). For 1915 until 1919 regional football was organised.

1916

City win the Lancashire Section of the wartime Football League – which comprised of all the Lancastrian teams of the period plus Stoke - and the Subsidiary Tournament (southern section) which followed. The southern section comprised of City, United, Oldham, Everton,

Liverpool and Stockport, with the other Lancastrian teams featuring in another section.

Billy Meredith returned to City, making his second debut in the 11th March 1-1 draw with Liverpool. A week later he scored his first Blue goal since 1905, as City drew 1-1 at Everton.

1917

In May Sandy Turnbull, cup winner in 1904, was killed while serving with the Manchester regiment in the trenches at Arras.

Hyde Road was used for stabling at times during the war.

1918

The end of the war came too late for the Football League to resume, but a final season of regional football was performed. After four seasons of regional wartime football, Eli Fletcher had made most wartime appearances for the Blues (133), closely followed by Jim Goodchild (130). United's Billy Meredith had appeared 107 times for City. Top scorer – by a margin of 50 goals – was Horace Barnes with 73 goals from 73 games.

1919

The first Football League

Maine Road's first league game saw the Blues defeat Sheffield United 2-1 on 25th August 1923. Max Woosnam was made captain for the day, and the Lord Mayor of Manchester was the guest of honour.

match following the war ended 3-3 with Sheffield United at Hyde Road on 30th August.

1920

All round amateur sportsman Max Woosnam made his debut on New Year's Day. Three years later he captained City for the first match at Maine Road.

King George V visited Hyde Road for City's 2-1 defeat of Liverpool. It was the first time a reigning monarch had attended a provincial football ground. He was said to be delighted with the result – well, he did have blue blood!

1921

City finished second to Burnley in Division One.

1922

Incredible plans to build a stadium capable of holding 120,000 at a site near Moss Side were announced. The 16 1/4 acre site, adjacent to a relatively minor street called Maine Road, cost £5,500. The builders Robert McAlpine worked with architect Charles Swain to design and build a stadium in two phases. The first phase opened in 1923. The second phase was never completed.

On 6th November 1920 a fire, started it is believed by a stray cigarette, caused the main stand at Hyde Road to be destroyed. Three stands still survived but Hyde Road's days were clearly numbered. Less than three years later the Blues moved to Maine Road.

The new Maine Road stadium was constructed during 1923, with the opening game coming in August 1923. According to builders Robert McAlpine, the entire stadium was constructed within six months.

Manager Ernest Mangnall was said to be chiefly responsible for the plan. It should be noted he was also responsible for United's decision to build Old Trafford about 14 years earlier.

1923

Maine Road, with an estimated capacity of 90,000, was opened by councillor Cundiff, the Lord Mayor of Manchester. Horace Barnes scored the first goal at the stadium after approximately 68 minutes. Sheffield United were defeated 2-1 before a crowd of 58,159.

1924

49-year-old Billy Meredith returned to City, making his third Blue debut in the FA Cup third round at Brighton. The Blues won 5-1 with Meredith claiming one of the goals – one fumbled in by the goalkeeper - as his own.

The next round proved the worth of Maine Road with a crowd of 76,166 paying a total of £4,909 to see Meredith & Co take on Cardiff. The game ended goalless, but City won the replay, giving Meredith his first City semi-final appearance since 1904. Sadly, a 2-0 defeat by Newcastle ended the

possibility of Meredith making a fairytale appearance at the two-year-old Wembley Stadium.

In May, for no obvious reason, the City directors refused to renew Ernest Mangnall's contract.

1925

Former Oldham Athletic manager David Ashworth led the Blues to tenth place in 1924/5. Unusually for the period, Ashworth had insisted on a 'get-out' clause in his contract with Oldham, which allowed him to leave if 'a better post' came along. Is that where Howard Kendall got the idea from?

1926

In January, City defeated United 6-1 at Old Trafford to record the highest derby victory of all time. In March they beat them again, this time it was 3-0 at Bramall Lane in the FA Cup semi-final. Unfortunately Bolton beat the Blues 1-0 in the final at Wembley, and then a week later City were relegated. Ashworth had resigned in November 1925, and chairman Albert Alexander took control of team affairs until the last few days of the season. 1925/6 was a typical City season!

1927

The club missed promotion by the narrowest goal average margin of all time – City's average was 1.7705; promoted Portsmouth's was 1.7755. Another goal would have swung it City's way.

1928

An average crowd of approximately 37,300 watched the Blues win the Second Division championship. This was the largest average in the entire Football League. Not bad for a Second Division side.

1929

Ernie Toseland made his debut in the 2-1 defeat of Bury on 20th April. He went on to make 409 appearances.

1930

Tommy Johnson, star player for a decade, was sold to Everton for £6,000, much to the annoyance of City's large support. During his career he had broken all City's goalscoring records. Today he remains second highest overall goalscorer with 166 goals from 354 appearances, and his 38 goals in 1928-9 remain the highest in a season.

1931

Billy Dale made his debut on Boxing Day after joining City from Second Division Manchester United.

1932

The Blues lose 1-0 to a Cliff Bastin goal for Arsenal in the FA Cup semi-final at Villa Park.

1933

A Dixie Dean and Tommy Johnson inspired Everton defeated City 3-0 in the 1933 Cup Final. The final was notable for other reasons – the players wore numbers for the first time (Everton were 1-11, City were 12-22), City wore red and white for the first time in a final.

1934

Eric Brook scored a wonder goal before 84,569 (to this day the largest in the provinces, and the highest for any club fixture) at Maine Road in the sixth round victory over Stoke. Two weeks earlier, the Hillsborough record crowd of 72,841 had watched City and Wednesday. A great deal of crushing and at least one death – the body was taken past Frank Swift and the others as they made their way through the tunnel – raised a few concerns over safety. However it would be a further sixty years before another Hillsborough disaster caused a major rethink.

In April, City defeated Portsmouth 2-1 to lift the FA Cup. Fred Tilson scored both City's goals. At the final whistle the 20-year-old goalkeeper Frank Swift fainted.

1935

The Blues finished fourth with manager Wilf Wild turning City into one of the strongest clubs of the period. A Maine Road crowd of 79,491 watched the crunch match with eventual champions Arsenal on 23rd February. It ended 1-1.

City's great captain Sam Cowan was transferred to Bradford City in October for £2,000. He remains the only man to appear in 3 City FA Cup finals (1926, 1933 and 1934).

1936

Arguably the greatest Irish player of all time, Peter Doherty, arrived at Maine Road for £10,000. He made his debut in a 3-1 defeat by Preston, although he admitted it wasn't his best performance by a long way. Preston's wily Bill Shankly managed to win almost every battle, nevertheless Doherty was to prove one of City's greatest acquisitions.

1937

With thirty goals from Doherty, City win their first League Championship. One of the best results of the 1936-7 season was the 2-0 victory over perennial challengers Arsenal on 10th

Sam Cowan and the rest of the city side take a look at the Sunbeam Silver Bullet at Southport in 1934. This car was taking part in trials at Southport for the British land speed record, after attempting to beat the world landspeed record in 1930. The fastest speed it ever achieved was 186 mph, and in 1934 the British record stood at 217 mph.

April. A crowd of 76,000 – some 13,000 more than the Manchester derby – enjoyed goals from Toseland and Doherty.

In August, a Manchester Liners ship was named 'Manchester City' in honour of City's success.

1938

Unpredictable City were relegated a mere 12 months after winning the title. They also reached the sixth round of the FA Cup.

1939

The Blues ended the last season before World War II in fifth place.

1940

Many players joined the forces, while others performed other important wartime roles. Jackie Bray and Peter Doherty became

PT instructors for a period, while Frank Swift became a special constable. Apparently he became so confused directing traffic at one point that he felt it was better to walk away and leave the vehicles to sort themselves out.

1941

Guest players were commonplace as regional leagues were set up. United's Harry McShane, the father of actor Ian McShane, guested in 23 games during 1940-41 – he even scored against United in one match.

1942

The wartime regional leagues became extremely complicated with clubs being allowed to pick how many games they played post-Christmas, provided they featured in eighteen or more. Unfortunately City

only managed seventeen games in the post-Christmas league as a result of Blackpool withdrawing from a couple of fixtures. As a result the Blues were not placed despite gathering nineteen points from seventeen fixtures.

1943

In July former Blue, Mick Hamill, died in tragic and mysterious circumstances. His body was found in a river.

In October Maine Road hosted a thrilling 8-0 international victory by England over Scotland. Joe Mercer claimed it was the greatest game he had played in. Frank Swift was the England goalkeeper.

1944

On New Year's Day City were defeated 7-1 by Bury at Maine Road. Jimmy Heale scored for the Blues.

In 1949, this illustration of the Main Stand frontage was a regular feature of the City programme

1945

City's worst run of the war period saw the Blues finish 47th out of 60 clubs in the post-Christmas North Regional League.

1946

The FA Cup was re-instated for the 1945-6 season. Games were played on a two-legged basis. After defeating Barrow, City beat Bradford Park Avenue 3-1 in the fourth round first leg, then lost 8-2 at Maine Road in the return – City's record home defeat.

1947

George Smith scored all City's goals in the 5-1 victory over Newport on 14th June (the latest finish to a season). The Blues won the Second Division title by four points.

1948

A crowd of 71,960 watched City draw 1-1 with United 'away' at Maine Road on 7th April. The Reds were using Maine Road following war damage to Old Trafford. A crowd of 78,000 had watched City's home derby six months earlier.

1949

Frank Swift retired at the end of the 1948-9 season. Unfortunately his replacement, Alec Thurlow, was taken seriously ill with tuberculosis (he died in 1956 at the age of 34). Eventually, Swift agreed to fill in until the Blues found a suitable replacement.

In November former German Prisoner of War Bernhard Trautmann made his debut despite protests from some supporters.

1950

City were relegated in 21st place. Former player Les McDowall became manager in June. One of his first signings, Roy Paul, made his debut on 19th August in the 4-2 victory at Preston.

1951

The Blues achieved promotion in second place. Bert Trautmann was the side's only ever-present. He was also becoming something of a hero to the City faithful.

1952

McDowall's City lacked consistency. They finished fifteenth in 1951-2, and started the following season with only one victory in the first sixteen games.

1953

City ended the season in twentieth place, missing relegation by a point. Trautmann was the hero once again.

In October City beat Hearts 6-3 in the first floodlit match at Maine Road. The estimated

The team and coaching staff group for a pre-season photograph in 1958

cost of using the lights was a mere £3 per game.

1954

A slightly improved seventeenth place brought a little encouragement for the fans, but it had been another difficult season. 17-year-old forward Joe Hayes had encouraged some supporters, while McDowall's tactical brain started to see possibilities with a new style of play. It was later dubbed "The Revie Plan", but basically revolved around a deep lying centre forward. Don Revie himself hated the system at first.

1955

The Revie Plan helped the Blues finish seventh and reach the Cup Final. Newcastle defeated them 3-1. Don Revie was the Football Writers' player of the year.

1956

Fourth in Division One was followed with a second consecutive trip to Wembley. This time City defeated Birmingham City 3-1 with goals from Joe Hayes, Jack Dyson and Bobby Johnstone. The Football Writers' player of the year Bert Trautmann broke his neck in a collision some 14 minutes from the end of the match. He played on, not realising the seriousness of the situation.

1957

Newcastle defeated City 5-4 in a topsy-turvy 3rd round Cup replay at Maine Rd. The Blues led 3-0 within 30 minutes, but in the second half Newcastle fought back and levelled with only five minutes spare. In extra time

CITY DECIDE TO APPOINT

THE news broke during the week that our directors have decided to divide the duties of team manager and secretary.

Mr. Wilfred Wild will, when the appointment of a team manager is made, confine himself to the secretarial work.

The change has come about through the pressure of administrative duties, and the directors believe that it is in the best interests of the club that a new appointment should be made.

Mr. Wild has filled the dual post since 1932, when he succeeded the late Mr. Peter Hodge, and during his reign the City appeared in two Cup finals. In 1933 they were beaten by Everton, but in the following year they took the trophy when Portsmouth were beaten 2—1. They also won the League championship in 1936-7.

Mr. Wild became assistant secretary in May, 1920, and secretary in 1924, having held the secretary-managership for 14 years.

Swansea Town are our visitors to-day.

Their side is drawn largely from the surrounding valley, which in the past has produced many celebrated footballers, and has been built up during the war through a policy of experimenting with local talent rather than employing guest players for war-time fixtures.

SECOND LEAGUE

NEW TEAM MANAGER

Goalkeeper **Parry**, who first appeared for the Swans in the early war years, returned from overseas service last summer,

PORTRAIT GALLERY

GEORGE SMITH
Manchester City's Inside Left

CENTRAL LEAGUE

and has jumped right into top form this season.

Centre - half and captain **Gordon Davies** is a local man who was playing for Swansea before the war and continued to give them sterling service throughout the war period.

Left back **Fisher** is a product of the Rhondda Valley, where during the war he was six days a week at the coalface turning out for the Swans on Saturdays to give his usual 90 minutes of robust football.

Centre **Roy Paul** returned to the Vetch Field from service in the Middle East late last season and in a few games proved that service had not slowed him up.

The programme for the 1-1 draw with Swansea, played on 19th October 1946, carried the news that Wilf Wild was to return to purely secretarial duties after fourteen years of acting as secretary-manager. Wild, second only to Joe Mercer in terms of success, was a major influence at City for 30 years, before he passed away still working at the club in 1950.

City made it 4-3, but then Len White scored twice for the Geordies.

1958

In February Frank Swift died in the Munich Air Disaster. He followed United into Europe as a reporter for the News of the World.

1959

Bobby Johnstone moved to Hibernian after playing 138 games for the Blues. He netted in both mid-50s Cup finals. A 3-1 victory over Leicester on 29th April preserved City's Division One status and sent Joe Mercer's Aston Villa into Division Two.

1960

Denis Law marked his debut with a goal in a 4-3 defeat at Leeds on 19th March. A month later Colin Barlow scored a late winner against Preston to save the Blues from relegation.

1961

Denis Law scored six in an abandoned FA Cup tie with Luton. He also scored in the replay, but City lost 2-1.

1962

The opening day of the 1962-3 season brought an 8-1 thrashing at Wolves...even City's goal was scored by a Wolves player! The 1962-3 season was destined to be one of struggle.

1963

A 1-1 draw in a heated and highly controversial Manchester derby helped relegate the Blues. New Red Denis Law scored a debatable penalty, while in the tunnel at half time Pat Crerand hit City winger David Wagstaffe: "I clouted him one on the chin as the teams trooped into the tunnel.... I'd become riled with Wagstaffe and my Celtic temper boiled up."

1964

Harry Dowd became City's first choice 'keeper for much of 1963-4, however by the start of 1964-5 he and Alan Ogley took it in turns to fill Trautmann's boots. The

Sir Alf Ramsey, ex-City star Matt Busby and manager Joe Mercer attend a function organised by City kit manufacturer Umbro. Between them the three men were managers of the current holders of the World Cup, the European Cup and the League Championship. Of the three, only Joe Mercer was to guide a team to trophy success again after this photo was taken.

Joe Mercer and Malcolm Allison enjoy a cup of tea on the day of Allison's appointment as number two to Mercer in 1965

Now it's big City TEAM shake-up

BY PETER GARDNER

KEVAN

NOW it's the big Maine Road TEAM shake-up. After the sensational double dismissal of manager George Poyser and first team trainer Jimmy Meadows, desperate Manchester City today turned their attention to the problematical playing side.

And here the changes in the side to face Coventry at Maine Road were equally sensational.

IN THE FIRST TEAM . . . goalkeeper Harry Dowd was dropped, reserve team centre-half Alf Wood played centre forward, and Glyn Pardoe displaced Joe Hayes at inside forward.

IN THE RESERVE TEAM . . . England inside forward Derek Kevan played his second comeback game after a 2½-month layoff through injury—at centre half.

This drastic team shake-up is the follow-up to the 2-0 home defeat by Crystal Palace yesterday, when it took the attack an hour to get in a shot at the Palace goal.

OGLEY BACK

England youth international Alan Ogley — incidentally ex-manager Poyser's first buy when he took over as Maine Road boss less than two years ago—for Dowd is the only defensive change.

The changes would have been even more dramatic had not David Connor passed himself fit at lunchtime after recovering from ankle and calf injuries yesterday.

With Irish international Johnny Crossan switching back to inside-right it made a four-change City line up.

Today's team was picked by caretaker manager Fred Tilson and temporary trainer Johnny Hart in conjunction with the board.

But they left young Mike Doyle at right half and skipper Bobby

I'm disappointed in Blues, says Tilson

CARETAKER manager Fred Tilson today told me he was very disappointed at his first full-length view of Manchester City's senior team in action, writes PETER GARDNER.

His immediate reaction on seeing the Blues play for the first time in two years was that the standard of football was not good enough.

Said Tilson, chief scout under axed manager George Poyser and two-goal hero of City's 1934 Cup victory over Portsmouth : "There is a tremendous amount of work to be done here."

And from chairman Albert Alexander came an emphatic denial that the former "rebel" shareholders group led by Manchester businessman Peter Donoghue, who now serves on the club's Development Committee along with colleagues Chris Muir and Michael Horwich, were behind the dismissal of manager Poyser and first team trainer Jimmy Meadows.

The chairman also said he knew of no directors who might also be resigning, adding, "There will be no repercussions from the present situation."

SHANK!

STAND by for the sensation of the season. It's my tip that Manchester City will go for one of Soccer's biggest names as successor to axed manager George Poyser . . . BILL SHANKLY.

The Maine Road bosses want a new image and are prepared to pay for it. A top salary could be offered to the Scot who has guided Liverpool to promotion and the First Division champion-

The poor state of City in 1964-65 led to the sacking of manager George Poyser. During his reign the Blues seemed destined to struggle and had even recorded their lowest ever league crowd at Maine Road – just 8,015 spectators.

legendary German goalkeeper retired at the end of the 1963-4 season. His testimonial was watched by over 48,000, with thousands more locked out.

1965

After a mediocre season (City finished eleventh in Division Two), Joe Mercer arrived as the club's new manager. He

quickly appointed a dynamic coach called Malcolm Allison, and the two tried to revive an ailing club.

1966

Joe Mercer popped open the champagne to celebrate City's Second Division championship. A Colin Bell goal at Rotherham had brought promotion.

1967

A season of consolidation ended with City in fifteenth place. They had also reached the sixth round of the FA Cup, losing 1-0 to a powerful Leeds side.

On 9th October Francis Lee signed from Bolton. Mercer told him he was to be the final piece in City's jigsaw.

1968

Mercer and Allison's team of entertainers won the League Championship in style. Neil Young was top scorer on nineteen goals from forty games, while 'final piece' Francis Lee had netted sixteen from thirty-one. Allison said City were so good they'd be the first team to play on Mars.

1969

Neil Young nets the only goal against Leicester at Wembley to bring the FA Cup back to Maine Road for the first time since 1956. Tony Book is voted joint Football Writers' player of the year with Dave Mackay.

1970

City become the first English side to win a domestic and European trophy in the same season. The League Cup and European Cup

New chairman Peter Swales announces his new management team of Ron Saunders and assistant Tony Book on 24th November 1973.

Winners' Cup proved City's position as one of football's greatest clubs.

1971

A vicious boardroom battle threatened to split the club. Mercer and Allison ended up on opposite sides and the disruption ended City's trophy winning days, although the Blues did reach the semi-final of the European Cup Winners' Cup, losing to Chelsea.

1972

Entertainer Rodney Marsh was signed for a record £200,000 in March. The side was disrupted to accommodate the player and the Blues ended the season fourth – one point behind champions Derby. The boardroom battles continued, although Altrincham businessman Peter Swales was trying to bring the factions together. General Manager Joe Mercer

moved to Coventry in the summer, feeling he had no real position at the club.

1973

In March, Manager Malcolm Allison left claiming he could no longer motivate the players. The Board chose former player John Hart as his successor.

On Friday 5th October 'peacemaker' Peter Swales became Chairman. In November, Ron Saunders became Swales' first managerial appointment.

1974

Wolves beat City 2-1 in the League Cup Final on 3rd March. A week later Ron Saunders made his greatest signing, bringing Dennis Tueart to Maine Road from Sunderland.

At Easter Peter Swales sacked Saunders as City's league position worsened. Tony Book became City's fourth manager in just thirteen months.

In the final game of the season Denis Law, who had returned to City on a free transfer from Tommy Docherty's United, scored his last league goal in the Manchester derby at Old Trafford. It was a fairly significant goal.

Stan Gibson, head groundsman, and drainage contractor Eddie Yates discuss plans to improve Maine Road's drainage during the summer of 1965

Roy Clarke checks out progress on City's new Social Club. The club eventually opened on 1st April 1966 and went on to become a very successful part of Manchester life until the 1990s.

Chairman Albert Alexander checks in the players from Borussia Dortmund prior to the friendly played at Maine Road on 11th August 1967. City won the game 4-0.

City director and future chairman, Eric Alexander, hit the headlines in 1970 when he set off on a drive of over 1,000 miles across Europe to Austria for the European Cup Winners' Cup final. Here Joe Mercer prepares to wave Eric and his co-drivers Alan Gordon and Harry Finlayson off.

Mike Summerbee, groundsman Stan Gibson, and Francis Lee photographed after a training session at Maine Road.

Chairman Albert Alexander is caught by the press shortly after a takeover bid was launched in 1970. Ultimately the takeover led to the break up of the Mercer-Allison partnership.

Maine Road shortly after the end of the 1970-71 season. The North Stand terracing is in the process of being built while the pitch is starting to be stripped ready for relaying. This image was taken from the Platt Lane corner, built in 1931.

Rodney Marsh signs for the Blues in March 1972. Helping with the transfer are secretary Walter Griffiths, team manager Malcolm Allison, and chairman Eric Alexander.

Kaziu Deyna and his wife Mariola pose for photos after Deyna's transfer from Legia Warsaw

Record signing Steve Daley arrives at Maine Road on 5th September 1979. Tony Book and Malcolm Allison seem delighted with their near £1.5m English record signing.

These boots were worn by Colin Bell during his last league game on 15th May 1979

1975

Colin Bell, arguably City's greatest player of all time, received a devastating injury in the fourth round League Cup tie with United. The Blues went on to win 4-0 but Bell would never again return to full fitness. It was a cruel blow.

1976

Dennis Tueart's spectacular overhead kick helped City achieve a 2-1 victory over Newcastle in the 1976 League Cup Final. Young PFA player of the year Peter Barnes netted the other, while Joe Royle, who had scored in every round

leading up to the final, had an effort disallowed.

The dearest season ticket for the 1976-7 season cost £29 if purchased before 30th April 1976. A similar ticket at QPR or Arsenal would have cost around £60. £8 would buy an adult season ticket for the Kippax.

1977

The Blues finished second to champions Liverpool, missing the title by just one point.

1978

City's average attendance reached 41,687; the second highest average attendance ever recorded at the club prior to the move to the City Of Manchester Stadium. The Blues ended 1977-8 in fourth place.

1979

Malcolm Allison returned to City as 'coaching overlord' to Tony Book. In March, Borussia Monchengladbach won 4-2 on aggregate in City's last European tie of the century. Earlier the Blues had defeated FC Twente, Standard Liege and AC Milan.

On 9th September Steve Daley became the most expensive footballer in Britain when City paid £1,450,277 to Wolves.

Groundsman Stan Gibson photographed with Rod Stewart on the day of Stewart's Maine Road concert

Fans of Rod Stewart await his appearance at his Maine Road concert

1980

After selling stars Gary Owen, Peter Barnes and Asa Hartford, among others, Malcolm Allison was sacked in October. Peter Swales felt the club would be relegated. He appointed another flamboyant character, John Bond.

1981

Bond's City avoided relegation and reached the final of the 100th FA Cup. Tommy Hutchison netted both goals in a 1-1 draw, and in the replay Kevin Reeves scored a penalty and Steve MacKenzie netted an incredible goal, but it wasn't enough. A Ricky Villa inspired Tottenham won 3-2.

1982

Work started on City's ambitious £6 million redevelopment of Maine Road. The idea was to build a replica of the North Stand at the Platt Lane end, and to replace both the Kippax and Main Stand roofs with white barrel-style affairs. In the end only the Main Stand roof was replaced, and even then it wasn't completed; the 36 private boxes that were to be suspended from the roof were never built.

1983

David Pleat famously jigged across Maine Road to his captain Brian Horton as his Luton side relegated City to Division Two.

1984

Billy McNeill guided a bankrupt City to fourth place in Division Two.

1985

Promotion to Division One was achieved in the last match of the season. David Phillips (2), Andy May, Paul Simpson, and Jim Melrose scored in the 5-1 thrashing of Charlton. Promotion was vital as City's debts were reported to be £4 million with interest costing £1,000 a day.

Following disasters at Heysel and Bradford, City were ordered to make the 9,702 capacity Platt Lane Stand an away fans only area for the start of the 1985-6 season.

1986

Captain Paul Power took City to Wembley for the first Full Members' Cup final. City lost a thrilling tie 5-4 to Chelsea. The attendance was 68,000; 7,000 more than attended City's first FA Cup final in 1904.

The Blues won the FA Youth Cup, beating Manchester United.

1987

City were relegated to Division Two, despite the arrival of Paul Stewart and Imre Varadi.

On 7th November Huddersfield were beaten 10-1 in City's largest league victory at Maine Road. David White, Tony Adcock and Paul Stewart each netted a hattrick, but the opening goal was scored by Neil McNab. Huddersfield's consolation was a penalty netted by former Blue Andy May – the Huddersfield fans in the near empty Platt Lane Stand did the 'Conga' in celebration!

1988

In June, Tottenham paid City £1.7 million for Paul Stewart.

1989

Mel Machin's side achieved promotion in a tense 1-1 draw at Bradford. Trevor Morley was the goal scoring hero.

On 23rd September, City beat United 5-1 in the 111th Manchester League derby match. Two months later Peter Swales sacked Mel Machin and after Joe Royle turned the club down, he

Peter Swales welcomes Billy McNeill as manager in June 1983. At the time Swales described McNeill as the best manager in Great Britain.

The Kippax perimeter wall is in the process of being rebuilt. Note the fencing used to segregate supporters in the bar area of the old Kippax.

appointed Howard Kendall. Shortly afterwards Kendall sold cult-figure Ian Bishop to West Ham.

1990

In addition to signing several former Everton players, Howard Kendall purchased Niall Quinn during the 1989-90 season. It was an inspired signing.

Former manager Joe Mercer died in August on his 76th birthday.

Kendall resigned in November to return to his 'first love' Everton. Fans' choice Peter Reid was appointed in his place.

1991

Reid guided City to fifth place in Division One. The final game of the 1990-1 season saw City relegate Sunderland. Quinn scored twice in the 3-2 victory.

1992

The Blues again finish fifth in Division One.

On 17th August City drew 1-1 with QPR in the first match of the new Premier League. This was also the first League match to be broadcast live on Sky TV.

1993

An embarrassing performance against Tottenham in the sixth round of the FA Cup leads to a Maine Road pitch invasion on 7th March. The game also marked the opening of the 'Umbro Stand', later appropriately renamed the Platt Lane Stand.

A disappointing start to the 1993-4 season prompted Peter Swales, via new general manager John Maddock, to sack Peter Reid. The season was only thirteen days old. Demonstrations against the Chairman followed.

Brian Horton was appointed following the match with Coventry on 27th August. He was the eleventh and final manager of Swales' chairmanship.

1994

In February after a long and difficult take-over, Francis Lee became chairman.

On 30th April, the terraced Kippax Stand witnessed its final match.

1995

Brian Horton was dismissed after City finished seventeenth in 1994-5. In the summer Alan Ball was appointed manager.

On 15th July Georgiou Kinkladze arrived in a £2 million three-year deal. Francis Lee, Jimmy Frizzell and Colin Bell had all been impressed when they went to watch him.

1996

City lose a controversial fifth round FA Cup tie at Old Trafford. With City 1-0 up and in total control of the match, United were awarded a highly debatable penalty. The Reds went on to win the tie.

Alan Ball's City were relegated after the final game of the 1995-6 season. After several depressing performances at the start of the following season, Ball was dismissed – during the game at Stoke he received abuse form both sets of fans. A managerial merry-go-round followed with Asa Hartford taking control (26th August – 7th October); Steve Coppell formally appointed (7th October – 8th November); Phil Neal filling in (8th November – 29th December); before Frank Clark was finally appointed.

1997

Clark's side looked encouraging at times during 1996-7, however the Blues had dropped to 22nd place in Division One by November.

These images show Maine Road during various stages of development.

Top left: classic Maine Road as it appeared between 1982 and 1992.

Top right: 1995 with the new Kippax and Platt Lane stands.

Left: residents protest as work starts on the new Kippax in 1994.

Bottom: the view from the top tier of the 1995 Kippax during final fit-out.

Groundsman Stan Gibson was not a fan of the Maine Road pop concerts of the '80s & '90s. Here he is with a bucket full of nails removed from the pitch after a 1993 concert.

Paul Lake's testimonial finally took place on Sunday 5th October. City drew 2-2 with United before 21,262 fans.

1998

Clark was dismissed and Joe Royle was appointed. Sadly his appointment came too late to save City from relegation to Division Two for the first time in their history.

1999

A thrilling, if somewhat nerve-wracking, play-off final with Gillingham resulted in City gaining promotion to Division One via a penalty shoot out. A crowd of 76,935 witnessed Nicky Weaver and Paul Dickov become cult figures.

2000

A second promotion followed as City returned to the Premiership in second place after a thrilling final match at Blackburn.

2001

Joe Royle's Blues struggled to make an impact in the Premier League and were relegated at the end of the 2000-01 season. Kevin Keegan was appointed manager after Royle's dismissal and quickly brought in Stuart Pearce as an experienced player and a key figure behind the scenes.

2002

Keegan's first season in charge ended with the Blues achieving promotion as champions of Division One.

2003

Maine Road's last season ended with a defeat to Southampton, however there had been plenty of highlights during 2002-3, including City's 4-1 victory in the last Maine Road derby match. The Blues also qualified for the UEFA Cup via the Fair Play League, and in August 2003 they played their first game at the City Of Manchester Stadium.

2004

The 2003-4 season ended with City's average attendance standing at 46,830, City's highest official average of all time.

2005

The 2004-5 season ended with Stuart Pearce as manager. Appointed caretaker manager prior to City's match at Tottenham in March, Pearce was given the job officially on the 12th May, three days before the last match of the season. Of the nine games played under Pearce that season, only his first game against Spurs ended in defeat.

2006

Micah Richards scores in the 94th minute in a one-sided FA Cup tie at Aston Villa. Sadly, despite City's dominance, the game ends 1-1, but the FA Cup run becomes the highlight of the season for most Blues.

LEAGUE MANAGERS

Lawrence Furniss 1889-1893

Joshua Parlby 1893-95

Sam Ormerod 1895-1902

Tom Maley 1902-1906

Harry Newbould 1906 -12

Ernest Mangnall 1912-24

David Ashworth 1924—25

Peter Hodge 1926-32

Wilf Wild 1932-46

Sam Cowan 1946-47

Jock Thomson 1947-50

Les McDowall 1950-63

George Poyser 1963-65

Joe Mercer 1965-1972

Malcolm Allison 1972-73 (Team Manager from 1971; Mercer as General Manager until 1972)

Johnny Hart 1973

Ron Saunders 1973-74

Tony Book 1974-79

Malcolm Allison 1979-80

John Bond 1980-83

John Benson 1983

Billy McNeill 1983-86

Jimmy Frizzell 1986-87 (continued as General Manager)

Mel Machin 1987-89

Howard Kendall 1989-90

Peter Reid 1990-93

Brian Horton 1993-95

Alan Ball 1995-96

Steve Coppell 1996

Frank Clark 1996-98

Joe Royle 1998-2001

Kevin Keegan 2001-2005

Stuart Pearce 2005 onwards

Vice-Chairman Albert Alexander managed the Blues on a temporary – but significant – period in 1925-6.

Nine of the thirty-two men to manage the Blues on a permanent basis were former City players. They are: Lawrence Furniss, Sam Cowan, Les McDowall, Johnny Hart, Tony Book, John Benson, Peter Reid, Joe Royle and Stuart Pearce. Cowan, Reid, Royle and Pearce also played for England. Cowan, Book and Pearce captained City to trophy success.

In addition, former Blues Ken Barnes, Fred Tilson, and Asa Hartford have had spells as caretaker manager.

In terms of most success, City's top ten managers are:

1 – Joe Mercer (ECWC, League Championship, FA Cup, League Cup, Second Division title).

2 – Wilf Wild (League Championship, FA Cup, FA Cup finalists)

3 – Tom Maley (FA Cup, runners-up League, 2nd Division title)

4 – Les McDowall (FA Cup, FA Cup finalists)

5 – Tony Book (League Cup, runners-up League)

6 – Ernest Mangnall (runners-up League)

7 – John Bond (FA Cup finalists)

8 – Vice Chairman Albert Alexander (FA Cup finalists)

9 – Ron Saunders (League Cup finalists)

10= Kevin Keegan ('new' Division One Championship)

10= Sam Cowan (2nd Division title)

10= Peter Hodge (2nd Division title)

10= Harry Newbould (2nd Division title)

10= Sam Ormerod (2nd Division title)

Note: Success rated in order of League, then FA Cup, then League Cup, with success in any of these rating higher than runners-up in any of the others.

Georgios Samaras and Paul Dickov celebrate a Samaras goal in the pre-season 3-3 draw at Wrexham on 19th July 2006. Notice the new home kit - City reintroduced blue shorts for the first time since 1985.

Modern City

Shaun Wright-Phillips in action at the City Of Manchester Stadium during the 2003-04 season

Captain Sylvain Distin watches Stephen Jordan's attempts to control the ball in 2006

Anelka has control while Belmadi watches during City's 3-0 victory over Sunderland on 21st April 2003

Benarbia weaves through Sunderland during the Blues' last victory at Maine Road

Apparently journalists said Riera found his debut tough going, but here he seems to more than have the measure of Neville and Ronaldo. The Blues won this derby 3-1 on 14th January 2006.

Stuart Pearce seemed to spend most of the 2005-06 season on the edge of the pitch

Joey Barton in action during the last Maine Road victory on 21st April 2003

A heavily bandaged Trevor Sinclair celebrates during the 3-1 City Of Manchester victory over United on 14th January 2006

Robbie Fowler celebrates with the fans in 2003. He netted twice after joining the Blues in January that year, with goals against Birmingham City (1-0 win on 16th March) and Sunderland (3-0 win on 21st April).